Crossing on Foot

Oliver Andrew

S.B. Publications

This book is dedicated to those who walked with me

By the same author
A List of Birds in The Gambia (with T Sims) 1969
The Stamps and Postal History of The Gambia (ed) 1985

First published in 2004 by S B Publications,
19 Grove Road, Seaford, East Sussex BN25 1TP
01323 893498
e-mail sbpublications@tiscali.co.uk

ISBN 1 85770 283 2

Designed and typeset by JEM Editorial
southerham@tiscali.co.uk
Printed by Fotolito Longo, Bolzano, Italy

Cover photo courtesy of Images-of-France

Contents

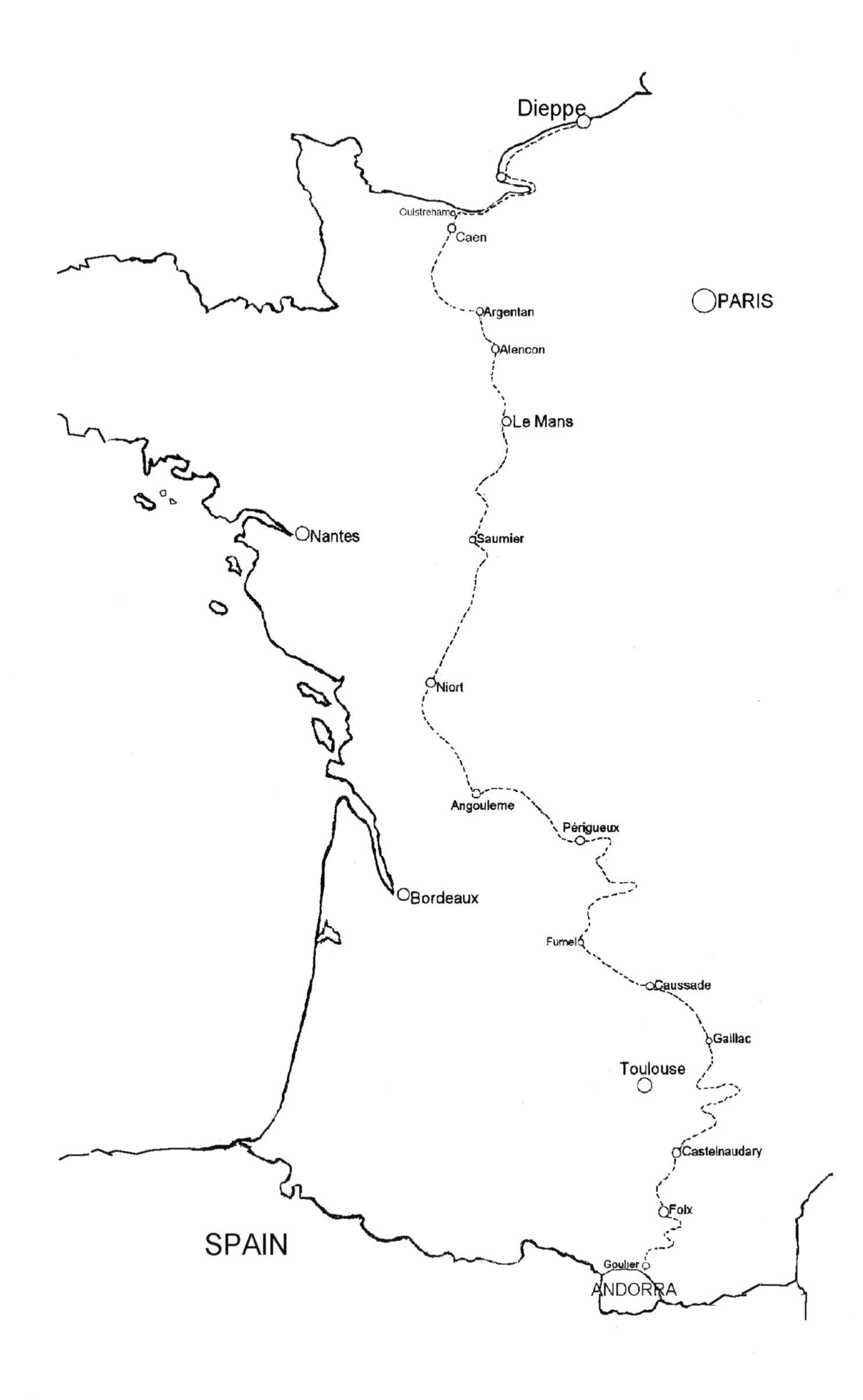
Dieppe
Ouistreham
Caen
PARIS
Argentan
Alencon
Le Mans
Nantes
Saumier
Niort
Angouleme
Périgueux
Bordeaux
Fumel
Caussade
Gaillac
Toulouse
Castelnaudary
Foix
Goulier
ANDORRA
SPAIN

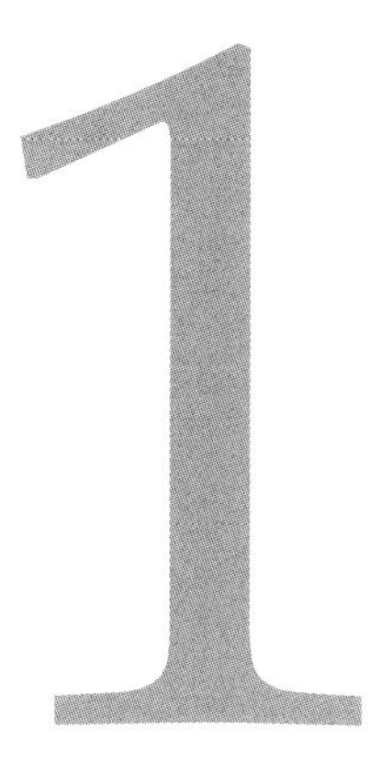

In the beginning

This is a story with several beginnings, many streams merging. One was the sluggish and prosaic onset of retirement at sixty, with its sense of the narrowing and accelerating future. Clearly I needed a shake-up.

A second stream – my family are walkers (My family *is* walkers? Buzz off, computerised grammar checker!). Not to make a political or environmental issue of it; not to breeze about in all weathers because it's morally superior to watching tv; nothing like that. But for pleasure, to be close to the countryside, and because we're nosy. As children, our holidays were walking – in North Wales, the Lakes, occasionally the Alps. My brother and his wife have completed the GR 10 along the Pyrenees – Atlantic to Mediterranean; my father and sister walked the Pennine Way in its early days; my parents walked round Mont Blanc long before that circuit became so fashionable; a family story credits my father and grandfather with taking part in the early 'trespass' walks on the Pennines; my great-grandfather used to walk thirty miles across the Pennines after work on Saturday night to court my future great-grandmother, and back again to clock on for Monday morning. My father-in-law, a conscript in the French army, and cut off by the German advance across Northern France in 1940, gathered a group of soldiers who were in a similar situation. They slipped through the barely-existent front and walked hundreds of kilometres towards home and safety in the South. By the time the Armistice was signed, and France partitioned, they were well on the right side of the demarcation line. What was I going to do to add to that record? True, Huguette and I once spent New Year's Day walking from Waterloo to York. But that was a distance of only ten miles in Sierra Leone.

Some streams were mere trickles: friends walked along Hadrian's Wall, up the West Highland Way, on the GR5 in Luxembourg, to Machu Picchu. I read accounts of walks to Compostela, Lake Rudolf, the North Pole. Slowly the stream swelled. But physical exploits seemed out. What I like doing is mooching, comfortable nights, a sense of the local life, sitting outside cafés watching, listening, sometimes talking. I needed somewhere I could understand the language well enough to enjoy all this. France imposed itself.

More than forty years ago I crossed France hitch-hiking with a friend. We saw Fontevraud with its tombs of the English Plantagenet kings, the straightest and emptiest roads imaginable, mad Americans, a golden oriole, threshing floors, dirty old men, countless fishermen, borage. We slept in haystacks, youth hostels, beach cafés, a bus shelter, on a railway embankment.

In 1964 I did it south to north on a moped. I saw women doing their washing on a sandbank in the river, a farmer driving an ox-cart, the Tour de France, a goshawk, Chartres Cathedral, countless pot-holes, rice fields, a horse-drawn hearse leading a crowd of mourners blocking a whole carriageway of the N8. Since then I've crossed France a hundred times, by plane, car and train; but to get close to a country you need to *be* close and move slowly. How much had it changed? How much had I?

The divide between those writers who find travel necessary, stimulating, addictive even (Greene, Waugh, D H Lawrence, Chatwin) and those who find it a terrifying bore because their art flowers in a familiar calm (Tennyson, Larkin) isn't just an English phenomenon, though it shows in us islanders with peculiar force. The thought that travel may change one in some unpredictable and scary way leads both to the 'travel broadens the mind' school, and to the sort of 'all-inclusive' holiday which isolates from all local ambience except sun, sea and sand. My view is that if you return unchanged except for being browner, fatter and poorer, you've missed the point. Some long-standing itch of curiosity needs to have been calmed or aroused.

My attempt at a solution is to travel in a familiar context (family, friends, France) and face the challenges of novelty a very small bit at a time. Age would give some advantage here, for once. I found other areas where it might, too. Nobody produces the stay-at-homes' classic 'squelch': 'What are you really running away from?' (The correct reply to this is: 'What have you got?') I thought of Nicholas Crane walking alone from Cape Finisterre to Istanbul (506 days) after only a year of marriage, and how he constantly worried whether the marriage could stand it. After thirty-two years' practice, I told myself robustly, I'll make bloody well sure mine does.

The objective, of course, would be Goulier in the Pyrenees, the village of my father-in-law's family, where we have a house, relatives, and friends: I would be sure of a warm welcome. American friends told me of the GR36 – English Channel to the Pyrenees. I got maps, guides, lists of hotels, bed-and-breakfasts, *gîtes d'étape*, (walkers' hostels). I worked out an itinerary, dates, sections on which Huguette and others could join me. I saw myself as Philip Larkin pretended to see himself:

But I'd go today,
Yes, swagger the nut-strewn roads,
Crouch in the fo'c'sle
Stubbly with goodness.

(he never went) with perhaps a Swiss Army knife and a baguette for all equipment. Well, all right, a razor. And wasn't there attraction in Stevenson's

Bed in the bush with stars to see,
Bread I dip in the river,
There's the life for a man like me.
There's the life for ever.

Aaaaarrrrrrgggggghh! No, indeed! Saner counsels prevailed. More experienced travellers suggested a change of underwear, a cagoule, maybe some money even. Still, I didn't intend to take a tent or cooking gear. Cooking gear, to France? And I didn't intend to look like those poor German girls you see in the Pyrenees, apparently carrying all their food for six weeks. With so many front-packs, back-packs, bum-bags, hand-bags, they can hardly move.

'Travelling on foot in fine weather and a beautiful country, in no hurry, and having at the end of my journey, an agreeable objective: this, of all ways of life, is the one most to my liking.' Thus Rousseau in his *Confessions*, here on his way from Paris to Chambéry in the Alps, and though it is easy to be uncharitable towards Rousseau ('agreeable objective' is a cold way of referring to an attractive widow about to become one's mistress) one can believe he liked walking. His last work was entitled *Les Rêveries du Promeneur Solitaire* (and just look at the force of that barely existent definite article). He takes an honourable place in the long list of those who've walked across France.

They've been doing it for ages, from Roman legionaries to Napoleon's soldiers. In all these armies, officers may have had carriages or horses, but the infantry walked. The barbarians, Suevi and Visigoths, who broke into France across the Rhine in the Dark Ages, moved into Spain. They were followed by the Vandals who, finding everything already destroyed or occupied by their predecessors, crossed Spain, the Straits of Gibraltar, and moved east into Tunisia. Most of them, including the women and children, were on foot. In the Middle Ages the Gypsies did much the same thing. Pilgrims to Santiago de Compostela walked, and still do walk. In 1212, for the Children's Crusade, thousands of children, led by twelve-year-old Stephen, from Cloyes, walked from Vendôme (and how did they all get there?) to Marseille, though Stephen himself rode in a cart. A very few walked back again. In 1792, volunteers for the revolutionary army marched to Paris from Marseille singing the revolutionary anthem - hence *La Marseillaise*, though it was written and first sung in Strasbourg. Nineteenth-century conscripts, before the age of the train, had to join their units by whatever means they could afford, so usually on foot. They were given a *feuille de route* with itinerary and stopping places marked so that they could ask the way and pick up the subsistence allowance of 15 centimes per league (the metric system takes time to catch on). I'm indebted to local historian Robert Reulle for the example of Alexis Pech 'Saïra', who walked from the Andorran frontier to Cambrai, near the Belgian border, at least 1000km, in the spring of 1849. 'I've arrived at my regiment,' he wrote home, 'but my feet are mangled' - as well they might be! And Alexis must be typical of many, many thousands. (Ten years later, in Italy, he was shot in the arm at the battle of Magenta - after which the colour is named - and died of gangrene within six weeks. That's another world).

Soldiers moved because it was part of the job, but civilians walked too. Craftsmen, such as masons and stone-carvers, had a well-organised system of hostels as they followed work about the country. Vagrants of all kinds, some harmless, some like the notorious Vacher l'Eventreur, who modelled himself on Jack the Ripper and walked forty to fifty kilometres a day to cover his tracks between murdering at least twelve people. Itinerant traders, wandering minstrels, monastery messengers, barefoot friars; nearly everybody who moved, walked.

In the mid-sixties, on La Crau, the vast stony plain east of the Camargue, and France's nearest thing to a desert, I spoke with a shepherd who was preparing the spring return to the foothills of the Alps with his several hundred sheep. The winter grass in La Crau was already drying up; he and his flock would spend some weeks journeying slowly along the mediaeval *drailles* (droveways) to richer pastures in the foothills of the Alps. And down again in the autumn, as it had been for centuries. But modern road-transport is so much quicker, that he must have been one of the last.

It wasn't until the twentieth century that people started to journey as a physical feat, an exploit. In 1900 the Austrian, Johann Hurlinger, walked 1400km from Vienna to Paris on his hands – I certainly wasn't aiming to match that. The first actual crossing, sea to sea, that I know of, was by Robin Neillands (who has written a very readable account, *Walking through France*, and also writes under the name of Rob Hunter) in 1987. Not all of these shared Rousseau's pleasure in walking, no doubt. But if they could do it, I could. And then there are the out-and-out eccentrics, like Marc Roger, who has walked 5000km round France, stopping to read in public his favourite works of French literature – in cafés, village squares, schools, retirement homes, town halls, housing estates…

And why not by bike? Obvious attractions would include fresh air, one's own effort, a speed suitable for contact. On the minus side had to be reckoned problems of security for overnight stops, and every time you visit a museum, or church; mechanical failure; being restricted to the roads, danger from vehicles. Travelling by car was ruled out. Cars are destroyers of place. Over-reliance on them makes the world a small collection of known familiar dots; the distances that hold them together, that relate and explain the differences, become a mere nuisance. We need the overall eye that melts (melds) this *pointille* into a picture; blue, green or brown spots, however pretty, aren't enough – we need to see people bathing in the Seine. I wanted to go slowly enough to savour places and people.

Moped? Been there, done that. Horse (camel, elephant or any other pack-animal)? A hugely attractive idea, but it raised problems similar to those for a bike. And they need feeding. And they're expensive. And what do you do with them afterwards? You can't just sell your horse to a French butcher, can you? Mrs Acland-Troyte and her husband, travelling by dog-cart from the Pyrenees to Cherbourg in 1886 and back, coped with all these problems. Her chapter on hints for beginners has detailed advice on how many litres of oats to feed your horse, and when. But that was before the car monopolised the roads. No, walking it would be. It has other advantages, too. Walking is an active sleep, a separation of mind and body like day-dreaming. And better than day-dreaming, it's another way of turning imagination into memory.

On a cold, wet, blowy day I found my way down some slippery steps to a basement where the Royal Alexandra Children's Hospital was running its Rocking-horse Appeal. After a startled moment the community fund-raiser produced, in under three minutes, a personalised sponsor form. Cynically I thought, sponsorship is collecting money for a good cause by doing something you were going to do anyway. But I knew better; as with telling so many people, I was looking for yet another reason not to back out.

Deciding when to go was no problem at all. Walking in snow is marvellous: I've been up the Glyders and Snowdon in January, and Glaramara in an April whiteout. But the enjoyment depends on being able to look forward to a warm dry place to sleep, and hot food; and slogging along in autumn mud and rain soon exhausts one's powers of delight. So summer it would be. Less to carry, too. Huguette claimed to be worried about the dangers: I might become addicted, and spend the rest of my life walking more and more slowly round Europe. Or insist on wearing boots and rucksack in bed. And what about nubile girl hikers, rosy-cheeked country lasses? Hm.... Fearlessly, I pressed on with preparations.

Friends and relatives warmed to the task of kitting me out efficiently. I must take spare pyjamas, a mobile, insoles, dubbin, one of those hats advertised as being a favourite food of elephants, a whistle, anti-snake-bite serum, distress-flares. 'Try those sort of ski-sticks they all have these days,' said someone. And why not an honest Zimmer frame, I thought sourly. 'If you took a personal organiser,' said my son, for whom sport has a strong technological component (skiing, cycling), 'you could programme in all the maps, routes, phone-numbers etc.' 'And,' added my brother mischievously, 'you should get one of those satellite guidance things they use on transatlantic races. Why, they pin-point your position to the nearest ten metres; you couldn't possibly get lost.' Here, as so often, a jokily far-fetched hare has been overtaken by that dull tortoise reality. The current issue of *Rambling Today* has ads for global positioners. And, so I heard, for 'military reasons' they're randomised – sometimes they give your position to within only 100 metres. (Remember the old story about the Government making sure every tenth condom was faulty, in order to ensure population growth?) Later I discovered that it wasn't exactly so. When the US Army first released the gadgets on to the market, they did indeed randomise the code, so that they were not as accurate as the army version. But civil manufacturers found that by taking three or four relative bearings, they could get an accuracy at least that of the military models, though more expensive. So don't worry: you'll be no more lost than the GIs.

But there's a pleasure in minimalisation; taking the least possible is an aesthetic aim as well as a practical one. It's a pleasure as well as a matter of size/weight/expense. Water-bottles, for example — you can pay £10 for a Swiss-made, one-piece, extruded aluminium bottle. Or you can buy tonic or mineral water in a lightweight plastic screw-cap bottle. I rejected things that were simply for putting other things in, such as soap-box, leather passport-holder, sponge-bag, slip-in case for alarm-clock etc. Instead I took those very light plastic bags you wrap your vegetables in at supermarkets. I took as many things as possible that had multiple functions. A giant plastic bag served as waterproof rucksack-liner and body-bag for forced bivouacs. Soap was shaving-soap and shampoo, underwear doubled as pyjamas. My stick, originally for dogs and nettles, served as a balancing pole, clothesline, snake-measurer, depth gauge, burglar alarm (see Appendix).

I began making lists: of things to take (plastic bags, torch); things not to take (too many pyjamas); things still to be bought; reasons to go slowly (creaky knees, conversing with the locals); reasons not to go at all (laziness, cowardice). The first time I picked up my complete pack I nearly fell over – the paper alone came to more than 12lb. I went through the list again, discarding spare socks, shaving soap, shampoo, cutting the maps to size. I decided against a mobile – cost, weight, recharging, the then patchy coverage of the French systems. By the time I set off, it was down to 25-28lb. The simplest attitude seemed to be to imagine being two stones overweight. OK, *another* two stones overweight. So that was all right then.

Paper was shrunk to maps, FFRP guides, diary and a slim volume of poems (Shakespeare's *Sonnets* first, then *In Memoriam*). I did read a number of books about walking in France, but didn't take any along. Some were clear but not on my route. One or two were supposed guides to walks that hadn't been tackled personally by the author – the information cobbled together from maps and leaflets. I could do this myself. Some were not intended as guides, but are excellent reading (Stevenson, Belloc, Hillaby, Crane). But others betrayed a merely superficial knowledge of France, and even a stupefying lack of curiosity. Some humorously played up a dangerous or unpredictable side of the journey, as though France were Outer Mongolia, French dogs were Hound of the Baskervilles, French people quaint, if good-hearted, peasants. Guided by these likes and dislikes, I set myself some rules. Don't overplay it, don't patronise, take your time, become part of the background, listen. Could I keep to them?

I did several longish walks, moving fairly fast, to break in new walking shoes, and to test a pain in my right side which the doctor thought was a potential hernia, rather touchingly called a 'thrill'. These walks also provided practice in listening to pub conversations. Four men came in, sat down to discuss work, different lagers, that time we all got drunk on Pernod – what you'd expect. Then: 'What about Ruskin?' 'That Ruskin in Despatch?' 'Rus*ker.*' 'No, Rus*kin*, you know, the art critic.' 'I didn't go to grammar school.' The conversation turned to cutting toenails for an elderly neighbour, and which washing powder to use for pullovers. Well.

The day came. Huguette drove me to Newhaven and put me down at the terminal. The ferry left at 8.30am. At that exact moment I was sitting in a graffiti-defaced train going back to Brighton, opposite a man with a greyhound cross, three young men with inadequate zit repellent, and some students complaining about an essay on Kandinsky. Best-laid plans etc! The weather had forced the Superseacat ferry to go to Boulogne instead of Dieppe. Boulogne was no use to me – another two hundred kilometres. Back home I spent the rest of the day working on Plan B, a more direct route (inland across the Pays de Caux, north of Rouen, across the Seine at Jumièges, through the Forêt de Brotonne) in case the weather held me up another day or two. The accommodation seemed more infrequent, and the countryside by and large less interesting.

But next day, May 24, 1999, was more as expected, despite one ominous blip. People-watching on Channel ferries is quite a specialised field; there were battered minibuses driven by tattoo'd electricians talking endlessly of money; young people in shorts, dreadlocks and metal bogeys; folically-challenged monoglots guarding cartons of twenty-four cans of baked beans; sad men bragging of how much they'd been charged for a Coke.

I sat next to a black American from Florida. The ferry going to Boulogne the day before had caught him out too, and he'd spent the night in Newhaven. 'Oh boy,' he said, laughing, 'there's more life in a graveyard.'

The blip came at Dieppe, where the staff insisted, ordered indeed,

The Superseacat from Newhaven arrives at Dieppe

that I use the passenger bus to get from the ship to the terminal. It turned out that this was to ensure that everyone went through the passport-control. I was very miffed that my 2000km walk should have to start with a fifty metre bus-ride. But then at last I was off along the quayside. In town I sent off cards boasting how easy it all was. Behind the castle, I found, with a thrill of delighted recognition, the first GR waymark, the red-and-white =. Disappointingly, the cliff edge itself is too dangerous for the public path, but following the waymarks, I stepped light-heartedly westwards along the coast-road verge.

May – Dieppe to Ouistreham

Day 1: I went quickly out of Dieppe, as I've known it since 1949. In those days the ferries used to arrive in the centre of town, towering over the fish-markets and quays. Boat-trains rumbled through the streets to meet them. The increase in road-traffic has meant an end to that; the harbour is now a fine marina where jetties are labelled after the town's most famous sons, sailors mostly. At the end of the Middle Ages Dieppe used to be the main French port. Its sailors are said, though on slender evidence, to have reached Sierra Leone in 1364, and there founded a colony called Petit Dieppe; others were early visitors to North and South America. The Parmentier brothers were the first (in 1529) to invent the ceremony of Crossing the Line. Ever since, sailors crossing the Equator for the first time, have been 'baptised' by Neptune, in a horse-play rite of passage. I have my uncle's paper (SS *Wangaratta*, June 11, 1923) certifying that he'd been 'doctored, ducked and dished' to become 'a true sailor'.

I was aiming for Pourville (7.5km), Vasterival (14km) or Quiberville (19km), depending. In fact I was at Pourville by 2pm. The only snag so far was the surface – all tarmac except for bits of verge. I found a tourist map of Seine-Maritime with hotels marked in places I'd not heard of (Quiberville), confirmation of others I'd doubted (Sotteville) and still others not marked here in places the guide did mark them. Was all my preparation going to turn out to be so patchy? There were a surprising number of ups and downs. The tarmac at last turned to track, then actual paths through attractive woodland. Vasterival by 4pm, it was far too early to stop. I passed little coves under the cliffs; saw a slowworm – glassy, semi-transparent. I was reassured to see, on approaching Quiberville, 'Hôtel du Casino' in huge letters on a roof, although was less reassured on closer acquaintance to find it decrepit and closed. But two others were open – why weren't they in the guide? I ate oysters to celebrate. **20km**

Day 2: I woke with sore knees to the steady roar of a downpour. I pulled back the curtains, though, to sunshine and a distant surf. The sore knees were equally illusory – this was the only time they were to make their presence felt. On the beach, men were fishing by tractor – driving across the sand to fixed nets. The local delicacy is *bulots* – giant whelks. Yuk! Decided on long coastal route (Plan A) instead of inland short-cut (Plan B) as accommodation was more frequent, the scenery better, it would make a good start physically and orientationally, and the places are more interesting. No walkers to speak of. In two days I'd seen one man and his dog, one jogger, and one hitch-hiking bag-lady. Kept stumbling – partly the footing, partly my big clod-hopping walking-shoes.

Veules-les-Roses (the roses were added in 1897) was about as dead as small out-of-season resorts can be. A clear chalk-stream flows down the middle of town, under former mill, out beneath the beach. '*Le plus petit fleuve de la France – 1100m*' says the blurb. Surely there are shorter streams than this? But French has two words for English 'river' – *fleuve* and *rivière*. They appeared, inexplicably within a few years of each other, in the twelfth century. *Fleuve* is a direct descendant of the Latin word for 'river' – *fluvius; rivière* comes from Latin too, from the word *ripa* meaning a 'river-bank', via *ripuarius*, 'situated by the bank', which rivers clearly are. This wider use still shows in Italian Riviera, and in French *riverain* – 'someone who lives next to'. *Sens interdit*, say the road-signs, *sauf aux riverains*. (Incidentally, the same Latin *ripa* gives us 'rival' – originally someone who shared the same riverside, someone whose interests were too close to one's own.) When a language contains two words like this, with identical meanings, it adopts one of several solutions. Sometimes one disappears altogether, like English *ycleped* (in favour of 'called') or one may be restricted; so 'stream' and 'burn' shrank as 'river' came into English – or an entirely new distinction may be made. This is what happened here. Dictionaries now define *fleuve* as 'flowing directly into the sea', and *rivière* as 'a tributary'. So the Veules really is the shortest *fleuve*! A fine example of how a language is not simply a collection of words, but a way of looking at the world.

All this coast carries records of World War II. Dieppe, and as far west as Vasterival, has reminders of the 1942 raid; further west, it's the Normandy landings. Here, it's the last 1940 fighting, when little pockets of stubborn soldiers still contested a long-lost battle – Rommel was on the Seine by June 8. 'They fell here on 12 June 1940 round their commanding officer,' says the little French Army memorial above Veules. And on that same day, in St Valéry-en-Caux, where I was now heading, Rommel's 60km dash north from Rouen captured 40,000

Chalk cliffs at St Valéry-en-Caux

prisoners, including the entire British 51st (Highland) Division, commanding officer and all.

The tracks ran between cows and crops (GR paths are always separated from crops and livestock); a clever herring gull had laid an egg safely in the middle of the GR. Gingerly knuckle touch confirmed it was warm. A small artificial pond on the cliff top where I stopped for lunch contained three *simbels* – plastic or wooden decoys to attract migrating wild ducks. In some regions they are an art form, with the best carvers widely known and respected. A route change signalled an extra kilometre. With a great thunderstorm coming up I dodged into a bus-shelter, not the last time I was to find them so useful. But the storm dawdled so I pressed on. Rucksack top pocket got a few drops and turned out not to be waterproof – from now on, it needed a plastic bag inside. Example No 1 of small-town France, what the French themselves call *la France profonde.* Into the café where I was recovering over a Leffe or two came an energetic delivery-man with a packet for *l'Impasse des Trimarans*; nobody knew this street. The *Syndicat d'Initiative* and Post Office were suggested, but the barmaid asked the key question: 'Who is it for?'

I was getting a clear impression that asking for a room for one person wasn't popular. Perhaps they'd rather wait for a couple. I was brusquely ushered out, indeed, in one place! The French attitude to back-packers, verging on an aggressive contempt towards vagabonds, caused amusement, annoyance and embarrassment during my walk. But there was an all-in price at the Hôtel de la Marine, where my plans caused a flurry of interest. I wrote up my diary and went over the day, speculating that these small incidents would gradually add up to more general impressions as subjects declared themselves; as not only the expected ones such as people and places, but unexpected ones such as saints, wood, donkeys, horseshoes, wash-houses were to. I was also surprised to find that my diary entries tended to get longer as the walk progressed – surely there's more to say at the start, when possibilities are endless? **21km**

Day 3: Lots of rain in the night, morning mist and spitting rain. St Valéry has a depressing number of deserted, or at least unused, houses.

It rained nearly all morning. I lost my hat, either left in field, or it blew off the cagoule hood. Ah, well, I'd a reserve. Two hares ran along the track. Waymarks were very poor for once; at one place the path appeared to go through a mile of hip-high sodden vegetation. So I detoured, past Paluel atomic power-station. Marsh Harriers. Small-town France, example No 2: road-sign in Veulettes to 'Mairie – Gendarmerie. In summer'. Problem of how to fill time: 20km at 4kph is five hours. A 9am start meant a 2pm arrival, rather too early. I would have to learn to dawdle, though that might be tricky in the rain. But did try to slow down, stop more, observe more of what was going on. Local architectural features included very neatly banded walls, three or four strings of brickwork alternating with flints. And thatched cottages have gardens along the roof ridges usually planted with irises. I was told that irises are the best for absorbing moisture. Even the slate roofs sometimes have these roof-gardens, though the usefulness in their case is doubtful – must be purely on aesthetic grounds.

I met a walker with cape, map-holder, IGN maps – all the gear. He was doing circular walks from a central base. Although he'd come across a Dutch woman cycling to Compostela, he'd met no more walkers than I had. Then a long muddy track up a surprisingly isolated valley far from any roads. *Gîte d'étape* at St Martin-des-Buneaux was fine, I was alone in a dormitory for twenty. To the *resto* in the village – two men and two women playing cards in the bar, two budgies lacing the hours with chirrups. As I was attacking an excellent rump-steak, in came the walker from this afternoon. He had been a scientific researcher before early retirement, now he sailed, walked, rode, ran marathons – oh dear! He was staying at the *chambre d'hôte* (B&B) next to my *gîte*, so we walked back together. He kept admiring the way I walked. I kept mentioning wife and children. An agreeable evening, though. The whole village seemed to be run by two women – one ran the *gîte,* three or four *chambres d'hôte*, a campsite, holiday cottages and a farm; the other ran the bar, restaurant, grocery and newsagents; the church was closed. **21km**

Day 4: I was enduring solitude much better than expected, perhaps because there was so much to do, look at, decide. More ups and downs.

Most places were either squashed into valleys, or thinly spread on the plateau. Names were misleading: *'.....-sur-Mer'* means overlooking the sea, not right next to it. Thus Hautot-sur-Mer, Ecretteville-sur-Mer, Vattetot-sur-Mer. Sotteville-sur-Mer does have access to the beach – down a dizzying flight of steps marked 'Danger'. Despite such obvious ambiguities in the language, the French see themselves as logical. *'Ce qui n'est pas clair n'est pas Francais'*, boasted Rivarol ('If it's not clear, it's not French'). But no language is logical, especially seen from the outside. Just try counting up to 100 in French; or look at the number of silent letters (*hôtel* – one, *doigt* – two, *baguette* – three). And the rest of any society is no better. The French have up to four separate police systems. They give road priority to the side they have poorest visibility on. They sow and harvest depending on the phases of the moon. They believe they are European, though they have an appalling record of compliance with EC directives (twelfth out of the sixteen members, above Greece, Portugal and Luxembourg, and well behind the Euro-sceptic Brits). They, or some of them, believe in copper bracelets against rheumatism, chain-letters, miraculous grottos, horoscopes, Ra-rings (only £20 – E30 – each, what a snip), graphology, palmistry, marabouts, clairvoyance, Nostradamus, intergalactic spaceships from the planet Myton, that what the Pope/the Bible/the Book of Mormon/the Koran says is incontrovertible, that the world will end in 1914, 1925, 1974, 1975, 1999, 2000..., that black cats bring bad luck. Some of them believe in more than one of these. We English see ourselves as practical and down-to-earth. But there's little practicality or logic in the way we wire up a plug or change a fuse, buy sawn timber, prove our identity or our rights-of-way. Look at the number of silent letters (buy – one, chocolate – two, knighted – three); we find unthinkable the idea of reforming our spelling to improve literacy. We adopt the metric system as though determined to show what a silly system it is, by allowing nothing between a unit and the unhandily tiny milli-unit, so that every measurement needs three figures (even the French have kept *une livre* for 500 grams). Our children are taught to manipulate metric measurements, but don't know their height, weight, distance, in them. We, or some of us, believe in horoscopes, graphology, clairvoyance, St Christopher medals, intergalactic spaceships that flatten patterns in our crops, chain-letters, that tickling your feet can be good for your liver, that what the Pope/the Bible/the Book of Mormon/the Koran says is incontrovertible, that the world will end in 1914, 1925, 1974, 1975, 1999, 2000…, that black cats bring good luck. Some of us believe in more than one of these.

Today's valleys were pretty and wooded; plateau was farm-land with cereals, corn, sugar-beet, peas and what I thought would be flax. Occasional farms were really isolated, three miles from their neighbours, surrounded by soughing beech-trees. Brrrrr! A splendid ginnel, and set of windy (and windy) steps brought me down into Fécamp – this used to be the mediaeval route for the town fishermen to reach the church up on the headland. Beer in *café* PMU – Pari Mutuel Urbain, the equivalent of the Tote. There are no bookmakers in France, so these are a combination of *café* and betting-shop. But all eyes were on the screen, and video-recordings of trotting-races are a poor substitute for conversation. **22km**

Day 5: Quick look at the Benedictine Abbey, home of the famous liqueur (it is open for visits, but you have to book well in advance), then along the front towards yet more up-and-down. Places in the valleys tended to be part tiny port, part posh holiday villas (all closed). Those on the plateau were suburban estates where I got lost – four times today – as nobody wants waymarks on their precious property. The main occupation was mowing the lawn; rumour has it that there are villages with no shop but a lawn-mower shop. They certainly were preternaturally neat. I sat in a bus-shelter to eat – it was the only dirty place, and the only public one, in the village. Most inhabitants seemed to disapprove of walkers – grown men wandering about with sticks and without wives. They checked their car-doors and fastened the garden gate. Women reacted more than men, whichever way, some actually smiled, but only the men spoke. I was nearly run down by a car in a pedestrianised street in Yport – pedestrians are clearly given priority, but sticking up for your rights costs too much. The only part of France where motorists voluntarily give way for pedestrians is Corsica. That does surprise the French, as it does me. Corsicans are notorious for not giving way for anything.

Then, at last, the path was along the actual cliffs – for the last few kilometres into Etretat. Sometimes indeed, there was little more than a metre for the path between the barbed-wire fence and a 100m drop. These are spectacular chalk cliffs, with dizzy formations carved out by innumerable millions of tireless waves. And there were people walking – couples, whole families as I came near Etretat itself.

Spectacular wave-formed cliffs at Etretat

Hundreds had walked up in the sunshine, to see the chapel and the cliffs. The reason for all this activity was clear when I walked into town – it was Whitsun, a public holiday in France. Despite my early arrival, all the rooms were full. I tried nine hotels; was offered a bridal suite, but the price, £80 (110 euros), didn't even include a bride. In the end I found a room for three. It must have been the last room in town. By five o'clock a crowd was besieging the Bureau de Tourisme, only to be told that the nearest vacancies were in Rouen, sixty kilometres away. Since that was where many of them had just arrived from, there was a near-riot. It was a typical bank-holiday crowd, men just sitting about drinking, groups of young people waiting for the real excitement to start, coach-loads of Belgians. Revellers woke me at 1am, 2am, 5am –

perhaps those without hotel rooms. I calculated I'd done 100km and climbed 1340m – almost Ben Nevis. **17km**

Day 6: Everyone was out – on the cliffs there were walkers, cyclists, horse-riders, joggers. A family cycle rally, an annual event according to the man handing out packed lunches, included cyclists of every age, and wheels of every diameter. Families were walking – there was even a girl on her own. As I walked through quite attractive woodland I could hear shotguns popping away to the right and all the rooks were cawing. I got closer and closer to the noise over the next 5km and it was clearly not just pheasant-shooting (unless the shooters were hopeless and the pheasants exceptionally dim). The path climbed out of the valley and all became clear – a clay-pigeon shoot was on. Men of all ages were taking their turn on the platforms to blast away at the 'pigeons', the ensemble giving a good impression of irregular fire from a small group of guerrillas defending a remote pass in the Hindu Kush. One curiosity: I was resting in a wood, on one elbow, when everything trembled. Earthquake? Heart-attack? No, simply two people, neither overweight, approaching. Can this be so every time? Is it drum-like effect of a falling water-table? Why did Red Indians need mats if elbows suffice? Must repeat. (I have; it isn't so. In what way was this unique, I wonder.)

Short-cuts brought me to Montivilliers, but it was yesterday's story again, *COMPLET, COMPLET*. Even the SNCF station was closed for the day. Luckily there was a bus to Le Havre (an excellent municipal service). On the bus, I was taken in hand by a little old anglophile – why do I say old? She wasn't much older than I. I moved my rucksack to leave her a bit of room, and she seized the chance to start conversation, Royal Family, Prince Charles, Toniblère, all approved of. Then town-twinning with German town – that was approved of as well. Then sport, she thought players playing abroad were good for the image of their native country, citing Petit and Anelka, then with Arsenal. I contributed David Ginola. *'Ah oui,'* she enthused, 'and isn't he good-looking!' Finally she approved of *métissage*, mixed-race marriages. I ventured that my daughter was married to a West Indian. 'Black?' she asked delightedly. After this, there was no holding her. She got me off the bus at the station, showed me across the street and on to the concourse, checked the train-times and the clock, showed me where to get my ticket, worked out how long I had to wait and which platform the train would leave from. By this time I could hardly stand up unaided. Slowly, resolution and independence returned with solitude. I rang Marion, Huguette's niece, in Rouen, bought a ticket, got on the right train. In Rouen, Marion and Thierry made room on their study-floor. We went out for a meal and some very enjoyable sight-seeing. Despite much searching and laughter, we failed to find the fabled *'Rôtisserie Jeanne d'Arc'* (Joan of Arc Grill in the English version of this deplorable urban myth). **24km**

Day 7: Train back to Le Havre, bus to Montivilliers to the exact spot I finished yesterday. Le Havre was rebuilt after the war, and is depressingly concrete by today's standards. We travelled through suburbs full of shops either closed or with metal grilles over the fronts. I seemed to be the only almost-normal on bus, except for elderly lady in suit, brooch, handbag. One woman seemed half-drunk, a grubby bandage round her head partly undone, with a long strip dangling. Her man was too sharp, disagreeably so, and smirked ingratiatingly. Most got off at the hospital. So that was it! No food promised this evening so I filled up at lunch in a *brasserie* where young women were taking their blue-rinsed grannies out for Sunday lunch – that included the lady from the bus. *Spaghetti à l'indienne* turned out to be what's still a rarity in France – a curry, decent though weakish.

Waymarks were awful. I was now on the GR2, supposedly running the whole length of the Seine, but certainly not followable here – I lost myself twice. In the I end abandoned the path and took the road. As I walked down its village street with my stick, I was stopped by a car full of hopeful revellers:

'St Vincent de Cramesnil?'

'Greetings my brother,' I wish I'd thought of saying, but just looked gormless I expect. They wanted directions to the neighbouring village. Not the only time my stick played the role of staff. I wondered what the punishment is for impersonating a pilgrim. This was not the first – and very far from the last – time that things weren't what they seemed.

My first *chambre d'hôte,* in a huge rambling old farmhouse. Like the farmhouse in St Martin-des-Buneaux, every surface was packed tight with ornaments – pewter dishes, jars of pot-pourri, vases of flowers, photos, sketches, souvenirs, antique lamps, doyleys… Bath! **15km**

Day 8: First-class breakfast. The usual guests were Belgians, very keen on cheese for breakfast, apparently, so I gorged. My opinion of Belgians soared. Normandy's the place for cheese, not only Camembert, try Pont l'Evêque and Livarot. It was rumoured that the bridge at Tancarville had been closed to pedestrians. The new Pont de Normandie cannot be reached on foot; the approach roads are closed to pedestrians, though motorists can get out on the bridge and walk up and down. Tancarville was already a four-day detour. The next Seine crossing upstream would mean another four days. I'd miss my rendezvous with Huguette. Well, I'd just have to find out. I took a short-cut I'd spotted yesterday, scrambled cheerfully down a hillside and immediately found waymarks – then lost them equally immediately. They were no better than the previous day's. I walked through a wood for 3-4km, emerging from behind a notice reading *'Danger – Vipères!'* The French have a thing about snake-bite. Some believe even slow-worms to be poisonous. The advice to take serum with me was from a Frenchman. But snakes kill no more of them than toadstools do. Then along the scarp above the Seine. This was the end of the Pays de Caux I'd been crossing since the start, though it's less bleak and shelterless here than in the north. I strode slowly out along roads with grass down the middle, saluting cattle and sugar-beet indiscriminately. The animals here were the same as anywhere – horses friendly, dogs officious, farm cats petrified, sheep panicky, goats sardonic, cows wide-eyed with that watchfulness they share with older babies and rabbits.

The French have a reputation, among Brits at least, for unfriendliness, xenophobia, a shoulder-shrugging unhelpfulness, and I certainly met examples. But two things today (and many others on many other days) belied that reputation. I phoned for a *chambre d'hôte* two days ahead. *Complet*. Could she perhaps give me another address in the village? *Pas de problème.* And when I rang there, the lady had a room, gave me detailed directions, was very keen that I should know the village restaurant was expensive but that there was a good pull-in for truck-drivers at Foulbec nearby, cheaper, better, etc. When I arrived at the Tancarville hotel, which is almost bang under the bridge (but double-glazed for quiet) they confirmed that the bridge was indeed closed to pedestrians. Hitch-hike? Swim? Again, no problem. Madame rang friends in Motorway Maintenance. What time was I hoping to cross? A van would pick me up in the hotel car-park at 9.30am then. Ah well, principles were made to be broken by such generosity. I sat on deserted quays, bird-watching in the evening sun. Then a marvellous meal in a restaurant overlooking the Seine, as the sun set. A group of business-men in suits using English as *lingua franca* drank water. Another group, of francophones, drank wine, laughed, took their ties off. Gloved waiters replenished my glass. **14km**

Day 9: Everyone was up and gone by the time I started breakfast. One table still laid (Ah, honeymooners, I thought) turned out to be for two German businessmen who had arrived in the small hours. Beautiful weather, so shorts for the first time. Lift across bridge as promised. The footpaths at the sides of the carriageway were being used as storage areas for repair equipment. The driver had no idea what I was up to, but the hotel had called in a favour, so….. He put me down at the far car-park, a truckers' stop. Women with improbable hair, and in micro-lederhosen, were discussing something through the cab windows with the drivers. The weather? I think not.

Along a dyke by river. Ships from Scotland, Malta, Belgium passed. Suddenly the path disappeared into a jungle – tussocks, trees, occasional

Pont de Tancarville

open patches of flints or jetsam, and nettles. All soaked in dew. Luckily it was early in the nettle season, they'd not yet reached that stage when an attack on one brings several of its colleagues toppling towards you. Good for bird-watching, but I was dripping after 4km when I finally got through. Dew brought up the smells – hay (not mown lawns as in the Pays de Caux), mint under the trees, wild onions in the woods. Young people, males at least, seemed quite forthcoming here: 'Hello! Walking's good for you, isn't it?' Try as I might, I couldn't detect a trace of irony. Foulbec drivers' pull-in OK. It had a joke stuffed duck made of two birds put end-to-end, the joint cunningly hidden by wings and feet. Even for a duck it looked smug. Conteville, with shops! I'd seen only one since Montivilliers, where they were shut. I sat on a public bench – again an improvement – and watched kids tricking each other, an older youth phoning to arrange his Saturday, grannies pushing babies in prams. How like and yet unlike an equivalent scene in England. Up from behind the roofs soared a white stork, and off up the Risle valley. I went to buy a bargain barbied chicken – yes, half would be fine, and yes, the storks arrived about ten years ago. A census last year counted sixty-nine; did I know that was more than in Alsace? Nobody was yet saying where they nest. Well looked after in *chambre d'hôte*, mothered would be more accurate. My legs still buzzing from this morning's nettles, I sank into a dreamless sleep.... **19km**

Day 10: ....from which boredom woke me. Another brilliant morning. High hopes of lots of storks on the marshes. None. Starting to meet evidence of war again, though here it's the Liberation of course. Small British war cemeteries attached to village graveyards, as at St Samson-de-la-Rocque; streets called after the Brigade Piron (the Belgian liberators of these coastal villages). Lost myself in Barville; the GR seemed to have changed status since my map. Wandered along minor roads for a bit. All villages are scattered as in Caux, but the plateaux are wooded, so everything's less visible. A church clock showed me that my clock had lost two hours somewhere. As I'd been blundering about cursing a lack of waymarks, and discovering I've not enough water, I pressed on. Water down to last few drops, and it was a hot day. Took to the Niokolo Koba swallowing technique I had used in Senegal (lots of swallows for very little intake). Couldn't decide whether the undoubted effect was only psychological.

I felt insecure for the first time as I sat on the verge in some shade. From a neighbouring house came a young man. He walked to within twenty-five or so yards, opened flies, pissed straight towards me. Myopia? Sexual invitation? Social commentary? Just another example of the French male's penchant for public urination? I looked determinedly away until he must have disappeared, when I disappeared too. But I felt the threat. And how easy to knock me down for the £500 and plastic I was carrying, then plead a road accident. Something similar must have occurred to the men in a dustcart later, who saw me lying in the shade by the roadside later, slowed down, and only drove on, smiling, when I showed signs of life. A Briton a year is murdered in France by persons unknown (as are 450 French victims; compare the fifty-five unsolved murders per annum in Britain). I came to a rather nice isolated valley with clear watercress streams, but the waymark painters are too keen on showing every monument, every view, every curiosity, so that the path zigzags quite inexcusably. Short-cuts of genius brought me to Gonneville, where I hoped to find a shop. None. Suddenly, at exit, there was a shack apparently made of old pub-signs and sheet-metal ads. And it was a bar!

Village bars are quite stereotyped. There's the barman, his family, one or two customers who know the others well. I discovered that my clock hadn't lost any hours at all, so I was well ahead of schedule. So over a second beer I joined in the conversation about fungi, then about retirement. One of the numerous attractions of abroad is that your accent is perceived as probably that of an outsider, possibly foreign, but never as a badge of class. Nobody assumes from the way you talk that you're rich, a snob, uneducated, homosexual, uncultured, a Protestant; nobody addresses you as 'Kev' or 'Chorles', or minces round the bar in a supposed imitation of your gait. Class distinctions do exist in France, though they are less general, less unconscious, and less resented than in England (where people don't use public transport because of who they might have to sit next to). A non-French accent cuts across these with ease. And this must help explain the sense of liberation experienced in France by so many English visitors.

Over the third beer they discovered I'm English. A van-driver at the bar immediately stood me a fourth on the strength of Man Utd having beaten Bayern in last night's final. Another man came in. 'Eh, Marcel, do you know we've got an Englishman here?' Marcel wasn't impressed: 'Bof, the English – Joan of Arc, Fashoda, Waterloo. And they drive on the left.' Suddenly the driver turned on him 'So who captured Joan anyway? The French, that's who. Who chaired the trial that condemned her to death? Cauchon, Bishop of Rouen, that's who.' I chipped in with two world wars. Taken aback by this vigorous display of learning, Marcel mellowed slightly.

An hour later I set off with clear route instructions, but was lost within 3km. Ad-libbed, ending with a scramble up a rough dark path suitably marked *Venelle de l'Enfer* (Hell Alley) to emerge magically in the centre of Equemauville. The *chambre d'hôte* was a typical Normandy farm round an enormous grassed courtyard. To village restaurant for meal – really excellent fish. I walked back past the village hall shuddering to rock music. What was my surprise to see through the open door, not spotty youths in jeans, heads nodding like turkeys, but a score of female pensioners bounding about to keep fit. **25km**

Day 11: Madame running the *chambre d'hôte* was really making a go of it. There were a dozen of us at breakfast, and she was hoping to attract more English tourists by taking a course in English, sponsored by the Gîtes de France organisation. I planned a route into Deauville along minor roads, and just as well, since waymarks were no more evident than yesterday's. A dog, whose owner had carelessly left the gate open, rushed out, barking enthusiastically. It was suddenly less enthusiastic to find itself in the road facing a stranger armed with a stick. Some diminuendo face-saving barks were followed by a rapid retreat.

Deauville is a real town – such a change after all those deadish villages. It's all boutiques here, rather than shops, but still.... Peroxided widows with well-valeted pooches; some English cars. Dearest beer so far (£2.20, three euros). The mayor of Deauville may be a countess, but that's no excuse. Parked outside the *café* was fifty-year-old ladies' bike (the bike, that is), with rear-hub three-speed, oil-bath for chain, skirt-guard and a carrier. Even as I scribbled this description its (male) owner claimed it and rode off. I looked in at the Syndicat d'Initiative, and bought a little brochure on local footpaths – nicely set out, coloured waymarks etc. Later I found myself following a very fetching combination of turquoise and royal blue. These paths are often marked out by municipal employees, so better and fresher than the GRs, which are done by local volunteers. But GRs are sponsored by Electricité de France, so it's always worth looking at pylons etc for the red-and-white dashes. Late picnic in sea-front gardens, despite signs forbidding it, watching girls pass, then along the celebrated duck-boards. Since Etretat, I'd taken to phoning two or three days ahead for accommodation, especially in villages, so was now booked as far as Caen.

Someone here certainly understood sitting-down. There were well-positioned benches – at the top of slopes, for example. I sat on them all, even if for only a few minutes, on principle. And later sat on the beach in Blonville, with sand and sea to the north – how odd! – writing postcards. One of those extraordinary French neighbourhoods where the building lots are parallelograms, and the houses haven't a right-angle between them, except to the vertical. Another sensuous bath kept me off my feet. I used it for physical audit; potential trouble-spots – knees and stomach – were perfect, back and shoulders fine, despite pack, feet in parlous state though, leaking blood and gunge, blisters

Greenwich Meridian at Villers-sur-Mer

first under sole, then on toes, now starting round heels, one toe-nail loosening under this attack. **20km**

Day 12: Was that all? It seemed more like twelve months! A brilliant morning and going to be hot, so I decided on a slow day despite the distance to be covered. In Villers-sur-Mer, which really is 'on-Sea', retired people in tasteful white duck and those natty nautical caps the French call *bobs*, or floral tops and bright slacks, were strolling on the promenade, with little rucksacks and the obligatory doglet. Heavy machines flattened out the beaches and skimmed off yesterday's litter. Sand is the stuff round here. Sometimes it rebels, invading gardens and today even the main road. Municipal workers were shovelling it up and putting it firmly back in place. Found I was sitting actually on the Greenwich Meridian, marked as such, despite the French lack of enthusiasm for an Anglo-Saxon line. They would have preferred the one through Paris to be the world longitude base-line, but conceded in 1911. At least, they gave up the claim to impose the Paris Meridian as a world-norm, but I notice that internal maps, for example French Government IGN maps, and some Michelin road-maps, still use the Paris Meridian. You may have to adjust your GPs – double check. For the millennium celebrations the French planted a line of trees right down this line, calling it *La Méridienne Verte*. Supposedly in 2100 it will be visible from space. A typically Gallic touch, imaginative and grandiose. Unfortunately, my route lay wholly to the west of that.

I took a splendid track up the back of Vaches Noires cliffs – sunken, flowery, shady, might be Devon or Dorset. Then caravan sites and company holiday camps. Down to Houlgate – poshish beach. Along the front to Dives, the Norman port from where William the Conqueror set sail on his way to invade England. He stopped over at St Valéry-sur-Somme further up the coast, which is how that town now comes to be twinned with Battle. By the marina was a CGT (Communist Trade Union) fair; a glimpse into another age almost, that of post-war collectivity. There were rings of seats waiting in front of the stage, tents with aperitifs and baguettes laid out on tables; a giant plastic chess-set and board, waiting for players. But where was everyone? Ten metres away in the marina were several hundred private-enterprise boats, with some owners polishing, pottering, looking nautical. Not for them the CGT fair. Over a beer and salad, and another beer, I saw no sign of life at the fair in the next two hours. And little actual sailing either. After lunch followed waymarks (aha!) over footbridge to Cabourg, along front, through town, into countryside and the marshes of the Divette.

And a good thing it was waymarked here, as the GR dodged about at right-angles to every obvious route, along reed-grown dykes, through nettles. I was button-holed by insistent hawthorn. Good birds – quail calling, honey-buzzard hovering. Sunburn, hay-fever, blisters. I arrived at Varaville exhausted. Another nice little family-run bar – cheapest beer so far at 90p, 1.25 euros). Then on to Petiville, well-named, with too much roadside walking for my liking. Street named after English liberator of village in 1944. Into Les Bas-de-Bréville, following signs for *chambre d'hôte*, as instructed on phone. Nobody was in. I sat for an hour in peaceful rural surroundings – cats, washing, garage doors open. Then I noticed that the house number was 35, not 34 as in the guide; 34 was a field with eleven cows. So I parked sack, set off to find phone. And sure enough, in the village 'centre' was my *chambre d'hôte*. Confused explanations all round. Returned, collected stuff still in the garden, went back to where I'd booked. God knows what the owners of the first place made of the unmistakeable signs of an occupation of their garden. Washed clothes, as every evening; socks and underwear regularly every two days, T-shirts whenever it looked as though they would dry overnight. Collapsed into bath, then listened to radio. Swifts low over the farmhouse.

'Un jour de sentier = sept jours de santé' ('One day on the footpath = seven days' health) says the FFRP slogan. And demonstrably more as a mere ten minutes' brisk walk improves one's mood for a couple of hours. Still, there must be other factors. My pattern was becoming clear – OK on the move, depression after stopping, but which passed with rest, gradual liquid intake, some food. Blood-sugar levels? Madame didn't think there was a public telephone in the village, but I was welcome to use her mobile. As a techno-peasant, I had to be shown how. Climbs totalled 2473m, equal to the height of the Pique d'Endron towering above Goulier, my destination. **25km**

Day 13: Change of weather to cool and clammy – with rain coming later? Short trek across countryside towards the Orne. A second *lavoir*, cleaner than the one I had noticed yesterday, but the same pattern – steps down from the street, roof, square tank, low standing-strip, iron bar across at height of a metre, feeder stream, drain. Now the tank was full of green scum, cans, frogs. Down by the river, well, the ship-canal really, I met a track between hawthorns, a 2km cool green tunnel. And the fauna! Cyclists, runners, joggers – some looking at chronometers, one accompanied by a fat boy on a bicycle yelling statistics – roller-bladers. On the water were coxed fours and water-skiers. All in expensive pulicised kit. Only me and some fishermen were scruffily not taking ourselves seriously. Bar at Pegasus Bridge besieged by Brits; it was only days till the fifty-fifth anniversary, due to start here at the very first house to be liberated in the Normandy landings, this one by advance paratroops. A veteran with a chestful of medals, curiously including one from 'Orlando, Fla', was keenly putting visitors right on points of detail. He comes several times a year, apparently.

Arrival at Pegasus Bridge, Ouistreham

Vile hay-fever again along canal. Even more cyclists on this bank. The only two walkers I passed, obviously Brits, looked studiedly at the hedge as I passed. What is it about one's compatriots abroad? The feeling is most neatly encapsulated by Kingsley Amis's Shenkin's Law, which says: 'Welshman A encountering Welshman B outside Wales will find that Welshman B is exactly the sort of Welshman that Welshman A left Wales to avoid encountering.' It's also true for English and French, and probably true for Mongolians, Costa Ricans, even Martians. But why?

Late lunchers round here, none of the Midday Witch effect of the Midi. In Ouistreham, red-faced, white-moustached squadron-leaders with chokers, and wives in twinsets and handbags, were still coming into the *café* for lunch at 2pm. But by 3pm the town, though full, gave off an air of post-prandial sleepiness. Into this, the arrival of a ferry-load of Brits, in their big cars, not knowing which way to go, some apparently believing they were in Caen, all nervously careful to keep right, threatened chaos and gridlock. The locals, in their small (because taxed less) cars, rose to the occasion, driving nimbly over lawns and pavements to clear the lines in no time. I dozed, then went out. In bars and restaurants, wives were keeping their husbands in order by waiting for the men to choose a table, then preferring elsewhere. I ate in a restaurant with many Brits waiting for the night-ferry. Two spent the meal explaining to the others where they had been at school. Suddenly I realised that more GB cars were passing and rushed to the terminal. Huguette said she thought I'd become paralysed when she saw me hobbling up on my blisters. Oh ha! ha! **14km**

3

June – Ouistreham to Argentan

Day 14: We sorted out equipment, guides, maps etc – no point carrying those I'd done with. Trying to find the left-luggage office at the ferry-terminal, we were just sent from one place to the other, but at the hotel the manageress agreed to keep superfluous bags till Huguette returned – yet another example of the obliging French.

Back along the Orne canal towards Caen, past old industrial basins with no signs of industry. Last 5km not very nice. We crossed bridge via a footpath within inches of HGVs. A wall of wind bumped us off our feet.

Under another bridge was an open-air brothel like that I passed at Tancarville and many others I've seen in the Midi. Luckily, only the haggling's actually in public, but it's not the main business that distresses so much as the concomitants – the girl pacing the tow-path looking suicidally depressed; the man sitting in the Merc waiting (for what?) while another man and girl bargained.

It turned out that after that first rather dry week, there was going to be a good deal of walking along rivers, almost always, for some reason, up. That was fine by me, despite the probability of much mud, as water *attracts*: fishermen, strollers, birds; and currents and water-lights are always new. But one attraction I would be missing was the sources. Despite days following rivers (Orne, Thouet, Lot, Tarn) in no case does the GR 36 reach the actual source. And sources are endlessly surprising. Merely of those I know, some, like the Rhine or Rhone, tear out in grey silty torrents from under glaciers and snowfields; some fall more demurely from green or silver mountain-lakes (Douro, Inn). Some (Vaucluse, Manifold) well up fully-formed, like knowledge ill-suppressed, from under limestone plateaux. The Seine has classical statuary and inscriptions to mark its beginning (a reminder that the Romans believed in the supernatural aspects of sources). Well, we still throw coins into fountains for good luck, don't we? The Loire rises on the slopes of the Gerbier du Jonc, in the east of the Massif Central. When I was there the little stream was trickling from a cattle-trough with a tap; luckily for the river someone had left the tap on. But none can match the Tagus. When I saw it one August no water at all was visible, just a huge monument, *El nascimiento del Tajo,* and a few square metres of damp clay, on which several hundred blue butterflies imitated a shimmering lake.

Meantime, we'd arrived in Caen. We found a hotel, siesta'd, went out to look round and eat. Caen has a road-pricing system. Vehicles pay by cash or card to raise the entry barriers to the semi-pedestrianised areas. The city was terribly knocked about in June and July 1944; it was the hinge of the Allies' strategy, but the two abbeys built by William the Conqueror and his wife escaped almost intact. Much rebuilding and restoration has taken place. And did you know that Beau Brummell, the Regency dandy, died in Caen, poverty, and 1840? **17km**

Day 15: Thunderstorm at breakfast delayed our start. Set off in mild drizzle, which turned to a steady downpour within two minutes. We tried sheltering under trees, road-signs etc, then simply gave up and got wet. Drivers were very ready to swerve to avoid splashing us. The rain stopped, we dried out as we walked. Fleury-sur-Orne: in 1944 the inhabitants of Caen took shelter from the allied bombardment in the limestone caves here. These have now been peacefully recycled for growing mushrooms in. And, an echo of an earlier war – the village used to be called Allemagne. Just as Saxe-Coburg was changed to

Windsor, the anti-German feeling of 1916 caused it to be renamed after Fleury-sous-Douaumont, a village which had been completely erased during the German attacks on Verdun. A fox crossed a field carrying its prey. A cuckoo was displaying on a tree. Church being completely renovated. Whole fieldful of parsley. Lots of very pretty river-bank. A group of thirty to forty teenagers passed us on some sort of physical outing, otherwise not a soul. Couldn't dawdle in this weather, so arrived early at our *gîte* in Clinchamps.

Huguette takes a rest

Confusion surrounds the word *gîte*, made worse in English by some dud explanations, even in guide books. The dictionary word means simply somewhere to sleep. The organisation Gîtes de France acts as an umbrella for a range of different categories of accommodation, using its logo – a map of France with a roof, an open window, and a Gallic cockerel – as a label of quality, a guarantee that the *gîte*, of whatever sort, is what it says it is, offers a range of specified services etc. Under this umbrella are:

Gîtes ruraux – houses to let for holidays, sometimes for a weekend, usually for a week or more. These are what are most commonly referred to as *gîtes* by Brits.

Chambres d'hôte(s) – B&B *à la française*. Also sometimes called *gîtes*.

Gîtes d'étape – hostels for ramblers' overnight stops. Basic accommodation with cooking facilities, and sometimes meals provided. They mostly double as:

Gîtes de séjour – similar, but for families, school-parties, groups, usually staying for some days.

Gîtes à la ferme – in farms.

Gîtes de neige – for skiing.

Gîtes panda – those in regional and national parks.

Some *gîtes* come into more than one of these categories. All appear in national guides published in the house green-and-yellow by Gîtes de France. Other networks, such as *Café-Couette* and *Clévacances,* and individuals, run similar *gîtes* in every one of these categories, as in my misunderstanding on Day 12, but they cannot use the Gîtes de France logo of course.

Ours was definitely a *gîte d'étape,* and there being no other ramblers, we had thirty-six beds all to ourselves. Huguette cooked a meal with supplies bought in tiny village bar/épicerie. Brilliant, considering. Found Beethoven Violin Concerto with Pinchas Zukerman on French classical music station. Slept well, too. **18 km**

Day 16: Fine at start, though rain constantly threatened. The Forêt de Grimboscq is a sort of outdoor centre for Caen; walks are sign-posted, there are even little carved signs for certain plants 'hawthorn', 'oak' even 'nettle'. It has plenty of shelters but only one walker. Where were they all?

Clear of trees by midday, then after 2-3km suddenly into what seems like a giant park, with grass mown. Tiny path marked 'Danger' for 1km, could only be dangerous for inexperienced townies, so clearly this was tourist country. We forced our way up through broom and gorse to cliff with a fine view over horseshoe loop in the river. There are several more of these. They must be one reason for the rather silly name – La Suisse Normande. Down unnecessarily slippery slope and along boring road past a GB car parked in a gateway with two elderly people asleep in the front, to Thury-Harcourt, where we admired rebuilt church, centre, war-memorials. Eighty per cent of the town was destroyed in 1944.

'Happy is the country that has no history' says the supposed old Chinese proverb and there are places, like Thury-Harcourt, that seem to have too much. But it would be an unreflecting, animal happiness; boring, not to be learnt from, unsavoured. Museums, cemeteries, memorials may be evidence of unhappiness, but they also celebrate resistance. They pin the past down; they're the facts that prevent our slippery imaginations slipping into madness; they're the public, iceberg, evidence of our private sunken memories. And one of the

A fine view over La Suisse Normande

practical uses of my walk would be to provide more striking, more colourful, more replayable memories and the facts that pin them – the sort of thing old men mull over by the fireside, or while basking lizard-like in the evening sun. Memories, as well as forgetfulness, are what keep us alive.

Rain started as we reached the hotel but, foiled, desisted. Swifts were nesting over our room. They came out from under the eaves so fast as to be barely visible. We sat by the river towards evening, watching weir, water and two species of wagtail. Dined on *tripes à la mode de Caen*, cider, Livarot – must support local produce! Huguette was properly pleased with herself at being able to keep up walking rhythm for three days. **21km**

Day 17: St Kevin's Day according to the French calendar. Not very long ago Kevin, or rather Kévin, was the most popular name here for baby boys. In England, for obscure reasons, it has become almost a joke. Luckily there is a saint of that name, as the French used to have, by law, to restrict their children's names to those that were officially recognised. Names of saints (Jean, Marie, Michel), names from classical history (Alexandre). Much ingenuity was expended on enlarging this small database. Girls' names were formed from masculine ones (Simone, Raymonde, Mauricette, Rémye); boys' names often compounded (Jean-Jacques, Paul-André, Ernest-Antoine). Pierre-Marie is a boy, while Marie-Pierre is a girl. A few (Mireille, Joffrette, Ossian) were slipped past sleepy or conniving registrars. It was not till 1968, when parents who wanted to give their daughter the unexceptionable name of Marjorie got the court to back them, that it became possible to go beyond the original list. The old system, which had been defended as a way to prevent the child being ridiculed, immediately fell apart. Children were named Jézabel, Salomé, Goliath (though of course Karim, Mohamed, Rachel etc). Sensibly the rules have now been tightened again. But even so there are clashes between strong-willed parents and registrars anxious to uphold the letter of the law. Guy Thomas dedicates his book, *In the Name of the Law*, about some of the absurdities of French law, to his grand-daughter. Her parents wanted to name her Cannelle (cinnamon); the registrar refused on the grounds that, although the law allowed names of fruit and flowers, it said nothing about bark. So the parents called her Myrtille (bilberry). Then there was the case of parents surnamed Renault who wanted to name their daughter Mégane. After eighteen months the courts allowed this, so at last the child had a legal name, and was eligible for family allowances and free schooling. But though it's very unusual to give a child an ordinary name mis-spelled so as to make it 'original' (Nickala, Karalin, Jenepher) as distinct from sheer illiteracy (Delores, Deidre), it's still possible to call a boy Clair – a girl would be Claire. So why not Mari or Suzan? Cruelty to kids, if you ask me.

Reverse of Day 15 – it started raining five minutes before we set out, heavier and heavier. Long before we arrived at the first village we were drenched. The isolated chapel of St Joseph was open though, so we regrouped. But there was no chance of drying out (little point, either). Guide marked a *café* in the village, but it was defunct. We stood under a church porch while breaks in the rain failed to materialise, then gritted our teeth and set off again. St Kevin must be the patron saint of wet clothing. Along grassy paths, slippery tracks in woodland, chilly wind, another 3km along river-bank in hazel coppice so thick it was as dark as midnight. We had thought we could cross footbridge into St Rémy and find a bar, but the bridge was private and locked. On we squelched, cursing, until the sun came through just as we reached the end of the wood. For the five minutes it lasted we stood and steamed, emptied out our shoes, wrung our socks, decided on a short-cut. So we trudged along the roads into Clécy, the main centre of the Suisse Normande. Our appearance at the hotel – sodden, muddy, dejected – was greeted without a murmur of surprise or dismay. We recovered morale and cleaned up, while sun and squalls, mostly the latter, alternated outside. Then we ventured out to see the village – a nice display of period postcards in little museum, with paintings by a local nineteenth century artist.

Local museums can be found all over France. They range from the tiny ones, such as this, which are sometimes just a room set aside in the Mairie, and have very restricted opening hours, through bigger ones such as the Georges Brassens museum in Sète, to first-class examples, like the Toulouse-Lautrec Museum in Albi, and the Musée Fesch in Ajaccio, both of which deserve their two stars in the Michelin guides. And the variety is extraordinary. Museums of local crafts and industries, traditional tools and machinery, armoured vehicles, hats, cinema, china, walnuts, ship-building, automata (at least two of these), kitchen equipment, the Resistance (several), pigs, dolls, apples and cider-making, the circus. Even, surreally, le Musée Imaginaire de la Sardine (yes, that's right). So, do the French collect more than the English? There is certainly an acquisitive, and 'What I have, I hold' side to their nature. thirty-five per cent of them admit to collecting something. But the craft and country-side museums are also explained by the fact that the change from a rural peasant society to an urban industrial one occurred a century or more later in France than in England. Even in 1940, fifty per cent of the French lived in the countryside and relied on their own labour and property for their food and income. In England it was five per cent. So anyone who wanted to record the changes had much more opportunity to collect, document, photograph; and was more likely to be aware of the importance of doing so.

There was a series of *guinguettes* – open-air bars – along the river, which must be very attractive when the tourist season finally gets going. Farewell dinner, as Huguette had to get back. Wine-label (Crozes-Hermitage, Jean Chapoutier) in Braille. This seems an excellent idea (nb The Wine Society had never seen another, when I contacted them later; the RNIB did know of a few examples). Apparently the raised dots can be done reasonably cheaply by silk-screen printing, so why isn't it more widespread? I thought for some time that M Chapoutier must have a blind relative but have since discovered it was a moment of empathy with a blind singer that inspired this philanthropic gesture. **16km**

Day 18: Up at 6.30am for Huguette's bus to Caen. *Boulangerie* open for 7.15am – we were the first customers. I returned to the hotel for breakfast. Grey, overcast. Set out at 9.10am so rain started at 9.15am. Suddenly it was less fun on one's own.

Deliberately I concentrated on where I was putting my feet. Up over some easy rocks in a thick soft driving drizzle. Sheltered in *lavoir*, now silted-up and muddy. How different these *lavoirs* used to be! With twenty or thirty women plunging their arms in, chattering, wringing, laughing, scrubbing, beating with their *battoirs* (dollies), passing the carbolic soap to a friend five places along. A group of sixteen-year-olds asked me the way. They were on some sort of orientation exercise, one with a map, two or three with bicycles, seven or eight trailing behind shouting to each other. Down nasty muddy (what wasn't?) path, following cows, to Orne. Then just like the previous day, a slippery track along bank. Blocked by fallen ash-tree, which took ten minutes to get through – wet branches and leaves are even wetter than wet grass. A few kilometres further, it was a fallen elder. This needed a ten minute detour through wet nettles. After that some sunshine, and even a rustic covered picnic area. More than one empty house had signs saying '*maison piégée*' – a booby-trapped house. If you force an entry you're likely to fall foul of a fixed shotgun or other nastiness. Is this legal? Probably not. In a notorious case a Frenchman, who had ingeniously booby-trapped his house, returned from holiday to find he'd been burgled. But the burglars hadn't opened the tempting cupboard containing the explosive. However, neighbours, who had heard strange noises, had called the police and the policeman had opened the cupboard. Four years in prison for the owner for assault and injury. There's an association which protects the owners on the grounds of 'self-defence'. I tried to work that one out as I walked on.

Into Pont d'Ouilly very early, but there was no point in pressing on till after Le Mans. I didn't want to arrive there with thousands of autophile Brits over for the 24 Heures (shortage of accommodation is reason enough). I found a cheap (because of thinness of walls, I realised) hotel room, where I mused on the differences between such close neighbours. We see the French as ungrateful, always wanting to have their cake and eat it, supercilious, xenophobic, too clever, hypocritical, paranoid, cynical, obstructive, triumphalist, mean, suspicious, passionate, arrogant, infuriating. They see us as hypocritical, mysterious, underhand, cold, supercilious, xenophobic, American stooges, isolationist, stand-offish, sexually deviant, obstructive, infuriating. Hm.

I was spending too much time lying on the bed staring at cheap wall-paper, so went out to walk by the river – canoeists, water-vole, fisherman with incredible extensible rod, 7m long at least, tip held right next to float, fairy-light tackle. But zero catch. Many of the fishermen were wearing the khaki uniforms and forage caps of Transylvanian camp guards. Why? Does it really fool the fish? I was getting a bit bothered by the absence of banks. I'd seen none since Caen, and as for cash-machines you might whistle. So it would be payment by card, about which there was no problem. Still no shutters on many houses. 'Thrill' in hip in some evidence this morning, but not uncomfortably or worryingly so, and not while on the move. Forecast was dull, cold showers, all weekend. **16km**

Day 19: Left at 9.10am – no rain! But plenty of clouds, an over-bright blue, and coolish wind. '*Il fait un temps tristounet*' (downcast, saddish) said the shop-assistant to a slightly gaga old lady. Ideal walking weather when it was not actually raining. Daily rhythm was still wrong, I was covering the ground too fast and arriving too early. Today this was aggravated by an involuntary short-cut. Some joker had put up a private-enterprise waymark, no doubt so as not to have ramblers rambling under his windows. The *lavoir* in St Philbert was the best yet, though still unused, and unusable without running water, but restored at least. And who was St Philbert? After Wales, France must be the country with the most, and the most obscure, saints – certainly as regards place-names. Some are called after historical figures, such as Martin, bishop of Tours, and patron saint of reformed drunks, who tore his cloak in two to share with a beggar; and Genevieve, who saved Paris from Attila the Hun. Some are called after saints from outside Europe, such as Cyprien and Pons, Tunisians both. But many are of purely local fame – Pardoux, Emilion, Ouen. Some saints have names odd to anglophone ears – Loup, Just, Poncy, Lager (which, even more oddly, produces Beaujolais). Some are simply obscure – Trojan, Adresse. There are St Chef (which means 'sacred head' but the French couldn't resist it of course); St Yorre (patron saint of thirsty people?), St Opportune (a convenient saint); St Amour (*the* red wine for that candle-lit dinner à déux). But St Philbert?

The cows with irregular brown blotches, including over both eyes, seemed to be Normandes; Blondes d'Aquitaine were easy to identify. I came to the Roche d'Oëtre, quite the finest of the cliffs dominating these river-loops, but after a bare quarter of an hour to admire it I was driven on by the stiffish cold breeze. So I arrived at La Forêt-Auvray far too early after all. As I was admiring the very nicely restored seventeenth-century market-hall, noticed a small restaurant. No possibility of a meal this evening, so I decided on late lunch. It was packed, but after some negotiation the patron put me at a table with ageing local curmudgeon. He was very good value. He had been a petty officer in the Navy, and had travelled everywhere. We discussed languages, how to learn them, who speaks which where in South America, how nice Tahiti had been in the 1940s. He told me about the patron's heart operation only a few weeks before; got me to guess at the nationality of the waitress – I guessed Greek, but she was Turkish – told me he'd had two hip replacements and was now as good as new. His unsteady gait on leaving must have been due to the calvados.

My conversationalist left after an hour. Behind me, a couple with a child were replaced by a Franco-British group of six. Nobody else, and there were more than forty of us, moved for another two hours. The patron had a certificate for the National Best-Tripe Competition, but I ate grilled lamb. Interesting grill system, with bars across the dogs to keep wood burning vertically, therefore fast, at the back, while the constantly-produced embers were raked forward into grilling area. I considered the accommodation problem for Monday night (the natural stop was a hotel closed on Mondays), then phoned. The booth was for coins only – this really was *la France profonde*. While I fought with piles of change, and a bad line, a huge tourist coach manoeuvred round the booth. It only just missed me and knocked the sign off the front of the PO. Public lethargy was such that everyone came out two minutes too late. I walked down the hill to château *chambre d'hôte* run by nice, straight, blue-eyed (and British) Mme Guyard. As well as the *chambre d'hôte* she manages husband, three children, two horses, dog, etc. She insisted I have a tv and, since it was pouring again, I watched French Rugby Cup Final. Stupidly slipped in the shower, but failed to break toe, wrist, tibia (though, looking back, this can have done my hip no good at all). **20km**

Day 20: I don't know who invented breakfast, but she deserves more fame than she has. What else so effectively counteracts the awfulness of waking, getting up, shaving, facing the day? I was given a first-class copious example in the former orangerie of the château, which has been revamped, and furnished and decorated with style and taste.

Then the path was all up-and-down; slippery squidge and stones alternated with slippery sludge and rocks. A stick was essential, not just for support, but for taking soundings. Through the deserted village of Le Vieux St Aubert – another obscure saint. It was founded in the eighth century and the last inhabitant went into a home in the early 1950s. Already the church walls and one or two other walls are all that remain. Wobbled about in woodland, some lovely, some not. In the afternoon, all the tracks had been messed up by some sort of motorised mountain-bike; the water couldn't drain because of the wheel-tracks. I slipped about and fell, swore terribly that I'd knock him off the vehicle if I saw him. Later I passed one on the road, like a very low scooter. The driver was about ten. Too many questions raised by this. I didn't knock him off after all. Later still I had to pick my way delicately over the guy-lines of a tent pitched right across the GR.

The Orne as a woodland river is quite as beautiful as any of the Devon rivers on the southern slopes of Dartmoor. But French rivers are only superficially like English ones – what that is French *is* like its English counterpart? Never mind the big differences, the small ones are even more revealing, since they seem so unnecessary. We hang horseshoes as a U (the Danes do too, I'm told, and the Italians) while the French hang them inverted, as do the Germans. The coarse-fishing close season in France is September to March, in the UK March 15 to June 15. Shop-names are different – WH Smith or Boots *v* Boulangerie, Chasse-pêche, or La Samaritaine (though this is changing). French streets are often called after important dates (rue du 4 Septembre) or abstract qualities (rue de la Liberté), English streets after fields (Brookside, West Meads) or the builder's mother-in-law (Beryl Close, Dorothy Avenue). French schools are called after great Frenchmen, especially if there is a local connection (Lycée Fermat in Toulouse, Lycée Corneille in Rouen, Lycée Kléber in Strasbourg) rather than the chairman of the local education authority famous only for his/her obscurity (you'll be able to find your own examples of this). Mothers' Day in the UK is at the end of March, ie nine months before Christmas – in France it's in May. French children have one 'truce-term' – *pouce*, the English have hundreds – pax, fainites, kings, bars, crosses, barley, squibs etc. English boys are told not to play with themselves or they'll go blind. French boys go deaf. Church-bells are rung the other way up, the dirt is not the same colour, garden tools have different handles, pushchairs face different ways, book-spines read different ways. And all that's long before you come to the beer. The two societies are like two pendulums not quite out of time. At unpredictable split-seconds they seem to hold the same rhythm, then more and more you see that they can't. But my aim is to revel in difference.

And the rivers? 'Bear with me,' as Herodotus might have said, if he'd been in PR or Customer Services. 'The digressions are part of my plan.'

Along the Lac de Rabodanges, '*aménagé*' as a playground, with water-skiing, cruises, bar. Just before Putanges, two curiously old-fashioned military vehicles crossed ahead of me, clearly part of the Normandy Landings Anniversary. I reached hotel under blue sky; ten minutes later it was raining. Bliss! The military vehicles were parked in

A small log pile near Le Mans

front of hotel – German writing on them, German war-time number plates, British tax-discs! Their drivers were dining that evening – they knew no French, not even *'deux bières'*. Brave, foolhardy or what? Still, they had some excuse, being over fifty. Not like a family I once saw, with three boys aged ten to sixteen, grey trousers and jackets, grey short-sleeved pullovers, private-school ties. They looked at each other shiftily when faced with the French trainee-manager, barely older than the boys, in the restaurant. Their parents looked away. Silence fell, then the eldest boy said tentatively, *'Er, manger?'* Why do we teachers bother I thought angrily. Good news 1: the Caen girls Rugby team had won the national championship for their age group; this is definitely not a rugby-playing area, the heartlands of which are down in the South-West. It's the equivalent of Gwynedd winning the County Championship at cricket. Good news 2: blisters nearly gone – my winter theory that only one thing goes wrong at a time may be right, as.... Bad news: the 'thrill' in right hip had become almost a twinge. **21km**

Day 21: Over breakfast I got chatting with the military-vehicle enthusiasts – a surprising amount of their stuff was either original, or copied by specialist suppliers, even the numbers were genuine war-time ones used on that type of vehicle, They had them printed on plastic overlay covering the UK ones. Apparently the French didn't mind. But they had to run on four-star petrol, though the engines were designed for 72-octane, and next year's insistence on lead-free would sink them. That was why they were risking this long run in France instead of the usual 100 miles per year just going to rallies. Off to Falaise next to visit the site of the encirclement of the German Seventh Army by the Allied forces. They were comparing 1944 photos with present ones. A nice example was a German tank backed into a shop to guard a T-junction. The shop is still there, 100 metres from the hotel, though closed, and you can still see the strategic interest of the manoeuvre. To my surprise, they'd had no trouble from the fact that the vehicles were clearly German; indeed young men were already waiting outside the hotel to ask them technical questions.

I left town past a memorial to *'M et Mme Bastard et leurs enfants'*, but the resulting warm glow didn't last long. After 10km 'thrill' was much worse; I was reduced to hobbling, and quite slowly at that. It was mostly road because of a short-cut missing yet another giant river-loop, but a very fine track led through a forest, with added Wood Warblers, to the surprising picturesque hamlet of Mesnil-Glaise. Then the countryside flattened out, this seemed to be the end of walking in a valley. There were wide fields of peas in pod – soon they would be scrumpable – with far views over rolling plains to the Forêt d'Ecouves, a day and a half away on the horizon. The weather was very changeable and unpredictable – in the end I just kept my cagoule on, so I arrived in Ecouché sweating and enclosed, smelling of wet rubberised plastic.

The Euro-elections were just getting under way. All communes are obliged to provide billboards for every party's posters, but many parties simply weren't bothering to use them. The usual hair-splitting among French parties about their stance was in evidence. The campaign slogan of one party – *'L'Europe pour la France'* – seemed disarmingly honest though. I sat in the village bar while the weather gave a further demonstration of its range. My hip was unnoticeable while I was seated, but a mere two beers later I was lurching spectacularly off through town towards the hotel. I crossed a plain under huge skies right down to the edge of the world. Fat pigeons sat on the telegraph wires digesting at top speed, then fell straight down on to the next course. The colours were those of the plain, too, green, some already yellowing into ripeness, huge grey sky-bands, dark horizons. But why so few skylarks? The hotel was fine. I had a rather posh room indeed, after they'd given me one already occupied by someone else. In the restaurant one dog, one mobile, one smoker, and there were only four of us! **21km**

Day 22: Right hip no better this morning, I could barely get downstairs. Some ghastly allergic-type bumps on neck, too, not very visible, I hoped. But I would have to see doctor about the hip. I turned down the offer of a lift and hobbled 5km into Argentan along the verge of very busy road. Dead animals on the tarmac included hedgehogs and a fox.

Colourful and busy market in Argentan which I couldn't bring myself to look round. More helpful people. In the tourist office I was given a list of local doctors, with advice as to the nearest. The doctor's receptionist welcomed me surprisingly respectfully and gave a prompt appointment. The doctor listened, rolled my legs around in a thorough way, diagnosed an inflammation perhaps the start of arthritis, showed me a model of a hip-joint, advised me to cycle as it uses a different hip-action, took my blood-pressure as a matter of course, expressed amazement that I wasn't taking any medication (the French are world-champion medication-takers: four times as much per head as with us). He told me I needed to rest – walking on, day after day, was no good at all. He wrote a letter of explanation to my own doctor and waived all payment on condition I sent a postcard either from England or the South of France. I did, of course.

So that was that then at least *pro tem*. I'd have to rest, and this change of plan left me flat. Would I be able to resume the walk later? How much not the same though! Had it all been for nothing? Why couldn't I have done it twenty years ago? Lunch at *brasserie* near station – several regulars first-named by waitresses, single women, businessmen in suits, single father with child, skinheads – all here to eat. Argentan is the birthplace of the painter Léger. I speculated while waiting why it is that so many poets and politicians (especially dictators – Hitler, Stalin, Alexander, Napoleon – but many others as well such as Gandhi, de

Valera, Ataturk) are outsiders, born and brought up on the very fringes of 'their' society. Painters and musicians aren't. Mathematicians come somewhere in between. You might expect the skills in which language is paramount, to be the preserve of centrally-born natives; but it isn't like that at all. Why not?

Aside from all this, the town gave me a most favourable impression of a society at ease with itself and therefore able to relax with outsiders. An impression that was only partly dissipated on the train by a pair-royal of discontented old biddies:

'But this is modern France, my dear!'

'Always the same thing…'

'I just can't tell you how many times…'

'If you only knew…'

'Why, young people today…'

Sulking with my own disappointment, I only just failed to scream. **6 km**

October – Argentan to Saumur

I wasn't able to clear my calendar for three months for a second time, so to avoid a recurrence of whatever the hip problem may be, decided to do two-three week sections, at different seasons.

I set off for chunk two via train and night-ferry. The train was late, but while waiting I spotted a fox scurrying through the buddleias on abandoned tracks at Hove station. The train reeked of the emotionally extenuated air of Sunday evening passengers, returning slowly and reluctantly to normal lives.

The taxi-rank at Portsmouth was shambolic. After ten minutes though I was offered a share by a nice girl (returning from Marseille, as it turned out. Evidently, when visible, I looked honest and trustworthy enough.

Day 23: Bus, unadvertised, from the ferry terminal into Caen through heavy rain; met train with five minutes to spare. I started this section as I finished the first, pootling through the countryside in a rickety train full of students, sixty per cent of the travellers with cigarettes, forty per cent with no choice. More bands of rain, but by 8.30pm I was in Argentan having coffee in the same bar as in June. There was the same comfortable mixture of customers, the same brisk friendly waitresses serving students and lorry drivers with even-handed aplomb. A friend who had read the draft of the previous section had visited Argentan on business and reported my favourable impression of the town to some inhabitants. They were astonished, and disagreed: 'No, this is just a boring provincial town,' they claimed. No way of reconciling these two verdicts but if you don't live there you may find the same as I did. Read paper while waiting for the weather to declare itself, and the sun to rise. Even *Libération*, roughly the equivalent of *The Guardian*, won't get Anglo-Saxon details right: *'La république de Nouvelle-Zélande'*, *' le general Clarck'*. Really! Warm with futile indignation, I set off walking. Bands of rain-cloud to the north and north wind. So everything caught up with me as the morning wore on – clouds, hip, lack of planning for tonight's stop.

I plunged steadily into a France more and more *profonde*. No horseshoes or *lavoirs*, but coin-operated phone-boxes, grass in middle of road, endless war memorials. Streams were clear, there were distant views across the plain to the Forêt d'Ecouves, even some skylarks. Blackberries were so ripe that many dropped off as I strode past. Villages varied – one had helpful signs to everywhere – hairdresser, sulky-maker, *boulangerie*. All were closed. Found the bar closed, with notice saying *'Fermé Mercredi'*. It was Monday, but hey! they both start with M. At St Christophe-le-Jajolet there was a huge nineteenth century church with external murals. It had been a shrine for local pilgrims. Now the door was locked. Five enormous crosses faced it across the fields and the precinct; there was an outdoor altar with seating for several hundred. All empty. Past *'Le char Keren'*, a small Sherman tank in a well-kept woodland shrine to commemorate the liberation of the village by Leclerc in the drive north from Le Mans to encircle the German Army at Falaise. No mention of any Americans. Field of unharvested sunflowers full of finches, chaff-, gold-, and green-.

The PMU bar in Mortrée was doing a roaring trade in scratch-cards. A series of not overbright young men scratched slowly, with much tongue-waggling and discussion, then rushed to claim prizes. Some came in more than once while I was there. My hip started to emit some strange twinges at about this point. Finally I limped into the *gîte* to find it open, occupied by twenty nine-year-olds and three teachers, but there was a room for me too. One of the children had found a fungus in the woods and brought it in to be identified. It was a *bolet*, a fungus with spongy underside. Was it a toadstool or a mushroom? Though hi/hello, gorse/furze don't bother us much, there is a general feeling that a difference in word must reflect a difference in reality. As with *fleuve/rivière*, on Day 2. Because some fungi called mushrooms are poisonous the boundary between edible mushrooms and poisonous toadstools is fuzzy, and we err on the side of safety. The French have a similar problem with *sureau* (elderberry). Nearly all *bolets* are edible and some, such as the *cèpes*, are excellent. Many French people can identify them; in case of difficulty, any chemist will tell you – *they're* trained. As a result, English-speakers don't eat many fungi, and are mycophobes compared to the mycophile French, Poles and Russians, whose languages offer no such pseudo-solution. The *bolet* was pronounced edible but uninteresting. We all, including the family running the *gîte*, ate together. The children behaved well, the teachers combined well (one shouted, one reasoned, one cuddled) to impose a socialisation expected, and consented to, by all. It was quite cold in my isolated building. I gathered twigs from the hedge to light a welcome fire.

Well, it definitely lacked the excitement and motivation of the first time; partly the season, no doubt, but also anti-climax, no novelty, no boost of physical or psychological exploit. Lurking fear of a second hip-problem. And less to look forward to, such as triumphant arrival on the square in Goulier. **24km**

Day 24: Very comfy night, alone in second building. Late for breakfast – the kids were just finishing. Luckily, the teachers had left most of the coffee. The *gîte* was very well equipped for school parties – bikes, ponies. Each child had been allotted a pony, and was expected to know it by name. I was thankful the WCs were normal, not the standard (bog-standard?) two-footprints-and-a-hole-in-the-ground, though there was the usual industrial-size drum of imperforate bumf. Clear cold morning with mist in the valleys. As the sun warmed the mist retreated to coiling snakes. I went down into that cold pearly silence. Drips. Farmers were out everywhere, mucking out milking-parlours, moving fences, laying down gravel. Rabbits, a red squirrel (no greys here, they arrived in England from the USA via Regents Park, in the nineteenth century and haven't reached the continent). I was barked at as usual by dogs, and even howled at by hounds. Hounds? In a regional park? But they were, and they even hunt here twice a week. Road signs ask drivers to be careful of them. At the Croix de Médavy there was another tank, '*Le char Valois*', and this time the American contribution had been properly acknowledged. This, with the Mont des Avaloirs a short distance to the south-west, is the highest point in Western France and for 250km in any direction. From now on streams would be running into the Atlantic not the Channel. Road-walking is hard underfoot, but the hopelessly waterlogged state of many tracks made an irresistible argument.

This is the forest primeval. The murmuring pines and the hemlocks,
Bearded with moss, and in garments green, indistinct in the twilight.

Well, perhaps not *quite* as primeval as Longfellow's Acadia.

There was an invisible hunt going on down to my left. Dogs, loud-hailers, shouting. On the road about 500m ahead appeared five animals, which binoculars confirmed as hounds. I approached gingerly, gripping my stick. But they were lost, and so pleased to see me. Fawning, grinning, drooling, wagging their tails, they followed me happily for hours, despite their colleagues being clearly audible away among the trees. Nothing got rid of them. I tried shouting, waving my stick, standing still for five minutes. The dogs had a big E shaved on their flanks, for identification. If I see a phone-box, I'll ring the gendarmerie and let them sort it out, I thought. Dogs, especially less friendly ones, feature prominently on a French walk I was to discover. In the end I walked at as even and boring a pace as possible. Relief – it worked.

La Roche-Mabile – nice little place. I read the village notice-board, as always. The catechism classes had been suspended *sine die* due to the death of the priest. The bar was open, the landlady smiling, though out of draught. A village wag, who may have seen me coming in, and scented novelty and a free beer, entered two minutes later. He entertained me and the landlady with a series of jokes and anecdotes, soon spotted I was English. Both he and she had been to Basingstoke, twinned with Alençon five miles from here. She worked in the bar for ten years, then bought it on January 1, 1975, so she was holding a millennium party for her customers – delivery-men, suppliers, accountant, '*Et vous, Monsieur*' (to me). That made three I was invited to. It turned out that the hunt employs a man to round up stray hounds after each day out. Wag recited Verlaine, then Little Bo-Peep in English, though he reached the end before I recognised it. More people came in; jokes went steadily down, both in taste and the age for which they might have been funny. But dawdling here, however agreeable, was a tactical mistake. When I finally reached St Denis-sur-Sarthon I found one hotel closed for good, one closed for annual holidays and the third anxious only to see my back (the French at their worst – formal, obstructive, contemptuous, as unhelpful as possible). So I staggered along the main road which carries considerable traffic, three, four, five HGVs in succession, for another 6km towards Alençon. At Condé-sur-Sarthe I passed a *lavoir*, disused of course. Someone had written a poem in felt-tip on Perspex and hung it up:

Il n'y a plus de fleurs dans le lavoir
Plus de bavardages, plus de rires dans le lavoir

There are no more flowers in the lavoir
No more gossip and laughter in the lavoir

The rest was no longer legible. But on the church was a sign to a *chambre d'hôte*. As invariably, I was given a warm and curious welcome, directions to the nearest food (a Carrefour cafeteria), and helpful information about the weather, local sights etc. Just like other *chambres d'hôte* in Normandy, the rooms were extraordinarily full. In mine, I counted on the wall - twenty-one pictures, two shelves, a wreath, two mirrors and a notice of the rules. There were three chairs, five small tables (on which stood four pots of flowers, one pot-pourri, three lamps, twelve books, ten miscellaneous objects), – oh, and a most comfortable bed. **31.5km**

Day 25: Beautiful day, thick hoar-frost, but clear, and sun warm. Smoke was rising straight up from the chimneys. Mile after mile of uneventful fields. In the quiet, robins sang, a car drove up a hill somewhere and down the other side, a dog barked in the next parish. At St Céneri-le-Gérei the first war memorial I found was to defenders of the castle besieged and captured by the English, in 1434, near the end of the Hundred Years War. One of the prettiest villages in France (that's official), St Céneri has other claims to fame; in the nineteenth century it was a popular resort for painters (Corot and Courbet both painted here) and, not least, the mayor is English. Ken Tatham, from Leeds, ran a restaurant here for eleven years, then became a French citizen in 1993 and mayor in 1995. An example to all Brits in France – become part of the local scene, even if becoming French is a step too far for most of us. Brits in France fall into several categories: full-time and part-time exiles, francophiles of all degrees, those after cheap living in the sun, holiday-makers who want to extend the holiday right round the year. But the rules are the same for all. Do try to keep in with the natives, do learn the language (not having a dictionary is like constantly having to ask what's trumps), do be seen to be making the effort; do what friends of mine did – they bought a house and land as one lot, then leased the land back to the former owner at a peppercorn rent. They also held a wedding-reception for one of their children, to which a coach-load of English guests came, and they invited the whole village. Do employ locals – of course you may get ripped off, but so you may in West Byfleet. Do join the *Comité des Fleurs* (unofficial) competing for the prize as the departmental *village fleuri*. Don't do what only too many do – form anglophone enclaves relying completely for a social life on their own resources. Don't shun the natives, or patronise them. (In one case I've heard of an English electrician was imported to rewire a cottage 'properly'. Of course, our 'proper' and theirs aren't the same. The French electricity authority wouldn't connect the mains supply.)

Out of St Céneri I took the GR 36 again, but the name for this region, 'Les Alpes Mancelles' is even more of a misnomer than 'La Suisse Normande'. It's on a level with, say, 'Greenland' (which really *was* given its name by Erik the Red to attract more immigrants) or 'The Steppes of Central Sussex'. The path was pleasant, even promising, for

3-4km over some empty hills, but then deteriorated into a flat country road through increasingly boring fields of corn-stalks. I got such a charming smile from one *factrice* in her PO van that I lengthened my stride for a whole kilometre, fantasising gently. While taking shelter from HGVs, in a small entry in Assé-le-Boisne I found it led to the best-preserved *lavoir* yet – clear water, wooden racks for drying the clothes, a roof. You could have used it right then. More GR brought me along a five-metre wide flood-plain between the river and a cliff, to which houses clung precariously, to Fresnay-sur-Sarthe. It's still horses, horses all the way, round here; trotting and driving especially in evidence. Indeed the logo of the Orne tourist board is a trotter, and all the horse-

As it used to be

A *lavoir* in proper use

boxes have a sulky-clip at the back. But the influence of Le Mans and its cars was becoming more evident. First hotel closed (again!), but Logis fine. **24.5km**

Day 26: Another frosty morning announced warm sun. Lizards and butterflies were out in force. Trouble with straps. I had thought my money-belt might hold trousers up but it was holding them down. I readjusted my clothing in a lorry-park, discovering as I did so that my flies had been undone all morning. Did everything up pdq and strode swiftly off into, I hoped, oblivion. Rang *gîte* for tonight's stop. Again clearly not wanted:

'We only do groups.'

'Well, I'm only one person.'

'But we can't heat the whole *gîte* for one person!'

'I don't need heating, I'm quite well equipped.'

'But we only do groups.'

'Merci, Madame!'

This ruled out the long loop east of Le Mans, so I had to replan the next three days' itinerary.

Past ostrich farm, all big eyes and bobbing heads. Farmers out again, hedging, ditching, driving about in old Peugeots with hen-droppings on the bumpers. All smiled. Drivers were happy to swerve for a walker, even white-van men. Horses and cows loafed in the sunshine. What had become of all that autumn mud I'd forecast? I re-jigged an image of autumn. The earth on its axis, wind in the trees, birdsong, cooling…. Directional and invigorating, autumn has all the astringency of a helter-skelter or flume.

St Christophe-du-Jambet on a scarp with a marvellous view to the south, but many of the houses were for sale including, deplorably, the bar. I improvised a hat with a knotted hankie, and picnicked in the sun. Duck-pond with tame ducks in a cage at one end, to attract wild ones; the hunting season had started. Flies – the sort that keep bumping into your face and bouncing off, not the sort that fly backwards just in front of your eyes. The sunken paths were festooned with cobwebs so I held my stick upright before me as though presenting arms or preceding an archdeacon. It was yet another use for the stick. Chris Baxter told me before I started: 'It's a very lonely life, you'll find yourself talking to your stick.' But that was still to be seen. My hankie and stick amazed the unsophisticated local dogs. Hip was quiescent; a loose toe-nail plastered on. Andrew's Law of One-Thing-at-a-Time works in reverse, too, when you're under pressure, so today, with everything else going smoothly, the muscles at the top of my left ankle were all suddenly aching. The GR took 15km from St Christophe to Beaumont, the road only 8km. And what do walkers get to see on this extra 7km? Fields of blackened sunflower stalks at this time of year, that's what. Perhaps 1km was agreeable. Is this just to keep walkers out of sight, perhaps? But these are the roads and paths of a hundred years ago and for many centuries before that. Some are now tarred but others still stone- or earth-based. We lost ours in the eighteenth century through enclosures and servility, so that people like van Hoogstraten can now sit on our birthright and sneer. In France rights of way passed directly at the Revolution from the Crown to the State. The French can walk their paths in pride and independence.

I passed more donkeys in a field, and in this mood wondered what's the point of them. The same is true, of course, for minority languages, another outdated technology. Mules and oxen have already gone. And if vegetarians have their way, cows, sheep, pigs, will all go the same way. Horses are for recreation, not for drawing or ploughing, so they'll survive as will other animals that we keep for recreation only – cats, increasingly dogs, Spanish bulls. We feel guilty towards those we exploit for non-emotional purposes. Who feels affection for sheep, geese or turkeys? Yet donkeys persist in a sort of limbo.

The standard pattern of French progress, of any change indeed, is stops and leaps. It's long been a truism to say that they prefer revolution to reform. These country areas will go straight from coin-operated public phones to mobiles. Another example – a real effort is being made in refuse-collection. Thirty years ago one just used to throw everything into the stream. Now sorting (glass, cardboard) is obligatory. They'll overtake us in this in no time (as in public provision for the handicapped, you'll see). Our voluntary system is quicker off the mark but fails at the point where only compulsion will improve things. Still, donkeys aren't stubborn asses for nothing.

Where were all the Brits? I'd seen only one GB plate since landing, though not many other foreigners either, and no walkers at all. Beaumont-sur-Sarthe turned out to be a nice little town ruined by permanent 5km traffic jams. HGVs from everywhere. The main street was hell on wheels. Roll on, the new motorway! I sat in hotel bar where men in their thirties were ordering *panachés* (shandies) and *monacos* (shandies with a dash of grenadine. Aaarrrgh!). Other mixed drinks are *perroquets, kirs, mauresques, tomates, diabolos menthe*. You'll have to try those for yourself. Introspected over a beer or two. Why was I doing this? Fear of growing old? Proving to myself I was still fit? Surely not; I felt about ninety-five plodding along with 15kg on my back and a rumbling stomach. It might be morally better than running away with an eighteen-year-old bimbette – or was it just that I couldn't get one of those, perhaps? Out to stroll round town. Fifty metres from the main road were little squares; a house where Rouault, the expressionist, lived and painted in World War Two; a lived-in castle. A poster showed the annual programme of events in-and-around. There were ten to fifteen per month. Some were restricted to certain groups – *Le Club des Aînés* (OAPs), *l'Association des Pêcheurs* (angling society) etc. But dances, concerts, drama, talks, roast-pig evening were open to all. At night double-glazing and metal shutters gave quite adequate protection from street noise. **22km**

Day 27: Good sleep but HGVs were back up to yesterday's level by 8.30am. Still, nice to see children going to school with those huge square French satchels, carried very high on the shoulders; men cycling home with a baguette in one hand. Breakfast in bar. A man came to clean the beer-lines with mobile line-cleaner, a little tank on a trolley.

Along cart tracks to start with. Today's flies were the ones that ride on your sideburns preparing to dive into your ear. I took a wrong track at one point. Along came a slightly bedraggled girl in a Renault 4 with a small child at the back. She slowed in fear and amazement, then passed me without catching my eye. Fifty metres on, I could see why. A rather tumbledown cottage, no dog, the door wide open – I could easily have taken everything by the time she got help. Then the HGV-infested N158, but I soon turned off towards St Jean d'Assé. A man in a white van pulled up alongside. Was I going to Compostela? Would I like a lift? No? Well, I must still visit Notre-Dame-des-Champs. He gave me careful directions then, in the middle of the road, we fell to discussing the shortage of priests. Round here, the *curé* does three communes, and house masses. But they're lucky. Much of rural France and most of housing estate France is now virtually priestless. The fall is of catastrophic proportions. There are hardly any new ordinands; no-one retires; dead priests are not replaced; services are carried out at irregular intervals, by lay volunteers; the sacraments are bussed in already blessed centrally.

Cars hooted and squeezed past. Was I sure I didn't want a lift? A meal? I hadn't the heart to tell him I'm not even a Catholic, but I did promise to visit the church. The village bar was quite well-frequented, though the staff were barely on the acceptable side of surliness. But it was all smiles in the PO. Was I going to Compostela? Perhaps it was my stick. Or today's shorts. I found the church in a farmyard. Very sweet, primitive murals, rather like Combes in Sussex, though some were barely visible. A mason was redoing the tiled floor, hired by Friends of Notre-Dame-des-Champs.

Log-piles were everywhere. So many logs can't possibly be for burning, but compare neatly with Diola rice-piles, or Fulani cattle in Africa, or Padaung neck-rings in Burma. The more you have the more important you are. You can still buy logs by the *canne*, a pre-metric measure, though now adapted (1m 30 x 1m x 1m; there are local variations). Like the *livre*, now 500gr. Huge grass snake in road suddenly in front of me. It looked dead at first but closer inspection showed not – it was inspecting me. Careful measurement (against my stick) revealed 'hugeness' was less than a metre. Just a tiddler, really.

Musing in this fragmentary way I arrived in La Bazoge. In the tiny, crowded bar seventeen people were finishing their midday meal and getting back to work (and six had already left). Most were artisans, though two were reps in suits. Old age in the countryside is clearly worsening but the young and middle-aged can find work as jobbing builders, electricians, carpenters, masons, plumbers (men) and in shops, bars, PO, insurance agencies, hairdressers, banks and town-halls (women). But what they're doing up is holiday homes for outsiders, often the retired. The farms are more dilapidated than ever and some, including many labourers' cottages, simply abandoned and falling down. This may reflect an increase in efficiency to make up for the population-drain away from the countryside. But with a European Common Agricultural Policy that was designed to support French farms, and which has succeeded brilliantly by and large, it seems paradoxical that some should not have been supported. It sometimes looks to city-dwellers, and especially non-French ones, as if French farmers are a privileged group. They receive heavy subsidies from the EC. They block roads, sack government offices, steal from supermarkets, riot, throw artichokes at the authorities, tip slurry outside the *préfecture*, place explosive charges to empty wine-storage tanks under the eye of an inactive *gendarmerie*. They ransack lorries importing Spanish tomatoes, or British lamb, they attack McDonalds with stones, crowbars and mechanical diggers. Much of this with impunity. And yet, if it's such a fine life, why aren't there more farmers instead of fewer? It's desperation, not greed, that drives much of the unrest. An ageing, mainly male workforce – the women get urban and clerical jobs when they can. It's a physically hard job; you're at the mercy of weather and chance. Social life is restricted to cattle-markets. In the Aveyron groups of farmers advertise for working wives from the Far East. La Canourgue has a festival weekend for the unmarried – to provide local farmers with an opportunity, often the only one, for meeting members of the opposite sex (as do towns in Ireland). But still the age rises and the farms and villages fall empty.

I finished my sandwich and beer, was on the point of leaving, when the landlady asked, rather respectfully, if I was going to Compostela. All became clear when she explained there had been several pilgrims passing this year. She and her husband were going to try sometime, though starting much further south. This was the only day I was asked the question.

I walked into Le Mans along an ever more pedestrian-unfriendly road. The verges were bare soil, littered with hubcaps, hawkbit, and plastic bottles; even grass couldn't survive. The bridges all have little footpaths at the side – there's evidently a law about this – but without approaches, so sometimes you have to clamber over the crash-barriers to use the footways. When I eventually reached a real footpath, I fell into step with a man leaving the supermarket. Proudly he showed me two new sponge-scrubbers. Just along the road we came to his house. The whole front yard was a towering heap of junk – old cars, fly-wheels, rolls of wire, bicycles, concrete-reinforcing rods, sewing-machines, fridges, corrugated iron sheets etc. I ran away before he could open the gate and it all fell out on us. And what did he want two sponge-scrubbers for?

Despite its good bus service and pedestrianised centre, Le Mans is a car-besotted town. I crossed streets called after de Dion, Bugatti, Bollée. One driver, keeping a close eye on a suspicious pedestrian (me), took his eye off the road and drove into a tree. How I laughed (it was a very small tree). 'In the Sarthe every 24 hours counts more than elsewhere' is the official tourist slogan. And tomorrow is the Le Mans 24 hour book-fair. Lots of hotels for once, though the first I came to was unavailable (but full this time, not closed). I spotted one on the map in rue du Père Mersenne, so I set off towards that. Mersenne was a seventeenth century scientist and mathematician, born at Oizé, just down the road, who was the first to see science as a collaborative advance. He got others to share their discoveries, was a lifelong friend of Descartes, went to visit Fermat in Toulouse, corresponded with Pascal, organised regular meetings that developed into the *Académie des Sciences*. A series of numbers, long thought to be all primes, though wrongly, of the form 2n-1, where n is itself a prime, is still called after him. Perhaps because of, perhaps despite all this, the hotel, which was cheap and wanted payment in advance, was very adequate (and the breakfast good). Felt strange to be in a city, so close to so many people; celebrated by going to Chinese restuarant. **29km**

Day 28: Rest-day, I thought. My feet were in worn condition with blisters and loose nails. I'd visit the book-fair and then see about pushing on south. Plenty of choice of accommodation for once. All signs to the fair were for vehicles. Stupidly, I followed them, round a long one-way system. But I did pass a stamp and postcard shop, where I bought an old postcard of Sète – still Cette in those days. At the fair I avoided the opening – coach-loads of children were pouring in – by going to a *café*. Inside was that early-morning seediness the French do so well; dodgy-looking men in leather jackets or mackintoshes with shoulder-straps, and even dodgier-looking women with hand-to-cheek Gauloises and hair dyed blonde, on bar-stools, looked resignedly at the grey daylight, sipped tiny black coffees or white wine, went over racing-form cards. Inside the fair was a variety well beyond just the books. I persuaded three nice girls at reception to let me leave sack and stick, although I wasn't an exhibitor. Several marquees, with regional publications much in evidence; authors of some national repute too. There were speeches of welcome, with that extraordinary formality that the French so deftly combine with *égalité* and *fraternité*: *'Monsieur le Préfet, Monsieur le Maire, Madame la Présidente des 24 heures du Livre, Mesdames, Mesdemoiselles, Messieurs'* (nice to be squeezed in at last). Outside schoolchildren had spread blankets on benches or grass to sell their textbooks (not school property in France). Stands of all sorts – the militant left, Rosicrucians, ornithologists and gay ramblers failed to enrol me. I was congratulated by a man who thought my stick denoted a scout-master. He congratulated me again, even so. A new persona to add to those of pilgrim, eccentric, tramp, probable child-molester-and-grave-robber-on-the-run. It was at about this point that I started to think of trying to work my notes up into a book. French books on walking tend to be severely practical (*topoguides* or 101 walks round Paris); up-in-the-air abstract (The Philosphy of Walking or Walking: a Thinker's Guide); or irredeemably up-beat, at one with Nature, a mystic happiness, striding out towards inner horizons etc. Not enough, I thought, about what the walker learns about the country he's walking through, as well as about himself.

Accompanied by constant blarings of air-tone horns, round the main streets went a parade of trucks, without trailers, painstakingly decorated with the most politically incorrect pictures – top-heavy girls in nothing but fishnet tights. Political correctness has hardly reached France yet, especially as a way of taking vicarious offence. No sign of what they were here for, though everyone else clearly knew. I walked out of town, which consists almost entirely of single-storey suburbs and industrial estates (Le Mans is France's nineteenth city in population, but is equal in area to the second, Lyon). Past a war memorial to the battle of Le Mans in 1871, the last in the Franco-Prussian War, when the Prussian Army simply rolled over the French, even this far west. But the French general here, Chanzy, was a fighter; despite losing this battle, a week later, when the armistice was declared, he was already regrouping his forces at Laval, 75km to the west, when the armistice was declared. The fighting retreat, at which the British Army so excels, is anathema to the gung-ho Gallic temperament of French generals.

> *Mon centre cide, ma droite recule, situation excellente – j'attaque! (Maréchal Foch)*
>
> *My centre is giving way, my right wing is in retreat, an excellent situation – I shall attack!*

Only Soult, backing along the Pyrenees in 1814 before Wellington's army, can be said to have mastered the art. But Chanzy certainly had the makings. I saw no memorial to the 10,000 killed in the streets here in 1793 when the Revolutionary army suppressed the Chouannerie, a peasants' revolt. I rang the *chambre d'hôte* – did I mind a very small room? Of course not.

Other walkers were becoming more frequent. Soon I arrived at the motoring circuits in an ever-denser crowd. I walked for miles through a huge car park. It was the 24-hour lorry race! Why pay for something you can see every day on the N158, or the A34, I thought sourly. Tents all over the car park and far out on to the airfield. The French were making themselves immediately at home, as only they know how – a temporary camp sprouts parasols, tables, chairs, geraniums. They sat round talking and eating; conviviality is a national art. Further on, the 24-hour circuit becomes the main road, or vice versa. I trudged happily along the sacred tarmac to the Arnage Turn, passing a small puddle in which were freshwater shrimps and two whirligigs. How can they have got here? At the *chambre d'hôte* I was warmly welcomed by M Brou, who poured glasses of wine, told me about a local monument to Allied airmen shot down in the nearby woods. He poured the rest of the wine then we went to see the monument and a new housing estate whose streets have been named after the aircrew. Their Halifax, from RAF East Moors, Yorkshire, was one of 100 planes bombing the factories and rail-yards of Le Mans on May 23, 1944. The crew consisted of one Briton, one Australian and six Canadians of whom two were of Polish descent and two probably of French. They are buried in the West Cemetery at Le Mans. What impressed the villagers was less how far they had come to fight, than their age. Not one was more than twenty-five.

Other guests were off to a wedding reception, so I ate with the family – a most agreeable evening. We discussed the value of their daughter studying Chinese (I was able to indicate Le Havre - the only university in France offering a course in Chinese and Business) and whether French Protestants have any equivalent to Guy Fawkes. They don't. M Brou was much amused that the construction of a nearby section of the new motorway was being held up by a colony of a rare beetle. Rest day? Huh! **15km**

Day 29: Apart from the 24-hour race, the Sarthe is not one of France's best-known departments, either to French or Brits. So it was nice to see at the Book Fair an exhibition of 100 Sarthrois of the Twentieth Century. It included some marginally Sarthrois figures, such as St Exupéry, who went to school here, and the Wright brothers, whose flight in 1908 at the racing-circuit convinced sceptical French aviators that they could control and direct powered flight. Incidentally, the first woman to fly in a plane (Mrs Hart O Berg, according to the books – but what was her name?) was taken up on one of these flights. There were some world champions, including Sandrine Plu (roller-skating) and Laurent Brochard (cycling); and figures better-known to the French than to us – Louis Rustin, inventor of *rustines,* adhesive puncture-patches, and Jean Bruce, creator, in 1949, of OSS 117 secret service agent (a clear pre-echo of James Bond). And before the twentieth century, Le Mans was the birthplace of Geoffrey Plantagenet, founder of the dynasty, and of Henry III of England and Jean II of France; strangely enough, it was not the only place to be so distinguished. Blois was the birthplace of Stephen of England and Louis XII of France. Much to my astonishment, Le Mans was also, I found, the birthplace of Arnold Dolmetsch. Born here in 1875, he was a musical craftsman who specialised in restoring and recreating seventeenth and eighteenth century instruments, and founded a dynasty at Haslemere, Surrey. The recorder, so much in evidence at primary school concerts and nativity plays, is virtually their re-invention.

I wrote all this down first thing in the morning as I had forgotten to yesterday. Weather grey and cold, countryside still grey and black. A cycling club in outrageously multi-coloured strip, like macaws, lightened the gloom. It was Sunday, so the fields were full of armed men. I read a notice about the shooting season; it was amazingly detailed. The hunting of everything, including snails, is regulated according to commune, site, species of victim, seasonal conditions, exact times of opening and closing. There are 1,900,000 licensed hunters in France. Landowners tend to be less protectionist than their English counterparts. *Chasse gardée* means only what it says; there's no threat as in 'Trespassers will be prosecuted'. Just don't climb over fences or leave gates open. How very sensible. And the hunters are very powerful. The *loi Verdeille* allows them free access to private land under a certain area, and all rights over game within in. That includes snails. All you need are a membership card and a shotgun. How very outrageous! In the 1999 Euro-elections their party, the CPNT (*Chasse, Pêche, Nature, et Tradition*), led by Jean de St Josse, got as many votes and seats as the traditionally strong Communist Party. Their chief electoral platform was to resist the European Court which had ordered the French Government to repeal the *loi Verdeille*. They haven't yet. More than forty-five per cent of French hunters claim that they kill wildlife out of a love of nature.

The locals here are very keen on not staring. If your eyes meet they look away immediately; but they're quite curious if they get the chance to look politely, not like some regions, where any unknown gets a serious ocular going-over. Through 2km of sandy hills, pines, heather, full of little weekend villas, caravans, shacks (shooting-boxes). Many had barbecues in full swing. In the villages, though, Sunday pm is even deader than Sunday am. Bars were closed, one or two teenagers hung about. I was in trouble for accommodation, as the *chambres d'hôte* are inconveniently spaced, and the key one was full. I walked round two and a half sides of a triangle and arrived *chez* Mme Hamandjian-

Blanchard for the warmest (in the face of stiff competition) welcome of this fortnight. 'No evening meals', so I'd brought half a roast chicken. Madame provided a laid table and … home-made rolls, pumpkin soup, a potato-and-courgette pie, a half-bottle of wine, fresh gingerbread made by her daughter. Not all *chambres d'hôte* offer evening meals, especially in the north of France, and out of season (I learnt to check when booking). Though there's often a restaurant not far away (more useful for motorists than walkers). But this was not the only occasion when I found that the rule was elastic. The luxurious room included plenty of reading matter. I was carrying Tennyson's *In Memoriam*, but no harm in a bit of variety here. Sank into a rich confident sleep. **24km**

Day 30: And breakfast was similar – ham, *rillettes* (local *paté*), home-baked rolls, ditto *brioche*, fresh orange juice, coffee, three sorts of home-made jam. Where in England is there a B&B like this for £25? (and it was one of the more expensive places that I stayed). Mansigné had a market, though only two stalls were up – clothes and fruit-and-veg. My appearance striding past caused a curious reaction in the women, ironic glances and smiles. Some sarky comments to idle husbands tonight, I guessed. My left ankle was again giving some pain. Filthy weather – mist, drizzle that stopped as soon as I put my cape on, and started as soon as I took it off. So I steamed inside. Birds in a rain-soaked elder had adopted a variety of strategies for picking the berries without being soaked in the resulting shower of cold drops. Blackbirds are big enough not to bother about hypothermia, they simply ripped their berries off. Smaller birds, like blackcaps, manoeuvred delicately to pick theirs from above. A black redstart hovered to peck at the ripe purple fans. But the sky cleared gradually, and by 1.30pm there was some sun and a multi-coloured sky. Nobody on foot, so cows and horses cantered across the fields for a closer look at me; I was handed on from farm to farm by barking dogs.

Arrived in Le Lude (on the river Loir, not the Loire) before seeing a walker, who then turned out to be only a hitch-hiker taking up position. No horseshoes for days, then today a gate with fifteen, all inverted. I was still itching to get on, despite swollen and painful ankle and my original decision to sit and to listen as well as walk. This impatience came from road-walking and constantly being passed by cars obviously going so much quicker. But it was not a competition. I had to match my rhythm to that of the country, like lovers. Le Lude is an attractive, sleepy little town – *loir* doesn't mean 'dormouse' for nothing. But the countryside is frankly boring, the weather was poor, the walking was hard underfoot, though I rejoined GR36 here, so perhaps something softer tomorrow. Like farms and village houses and hotels, too many shops in these small towns were closed and for sale. But someone would try. Of the 1,200,000 French who want to start their own business, forty-six per cent want to go into shop-keeping ('a nation of what?' did I hear somebody ask?). And the good ones may succeed. An average *cafetier-buraliste,* running a *café* with a state tobacco concession, earns 3,000 euros per month (£25,000 pa). Others who seem to be doing well are hairdressers and bakers.

In accordance with tradition, the first hotel was closed – but the other was open. Rested my feet, then went out for an appetizer. In the PMU bar a prim, efficient-looking lady took two minutes to fill my glass with froth. The girl assistant took a mere fifteen seconds to apologise, fill my glass, offer me another free, clear the pump. I phoned home from outside the abandoned station building (even the tracks had been taken up except those across the road. The SNCF owns the tracks and will only remove them where it's easy to do so). My maps must be the last place these railways existed. Good meal at the hotel – varied, original, plenty of vegetables; the waiter (Chinese) knew how to inform and how to flatter. He dealt imperturbably, in English, with two Germans who had no French at all. **16km**

Day 31: Breakfast news on local tv – pressure-groups of MPs, regional and county councillors, want more aid from Brussels. The average aid per head in this region, the Pays de la Loire, is only two thirds of the national average. Would this even be known in England? Who'd use it to protest? Local councils? MEPs? Weather grey and cold as before, until 9.30am when the north-east breeze dropped and sun shone for several hours. I stopped for a coffee in a village shop. The owner served me what was clearly some of her own breakfast, but it was hot and strong and did what matters. Feet were behaving well so I decided on route that would enable me to do a long or short day, depending. Sat down by roadside hydrant for a bite of chocolate, and found the familiar GR waymark there. So I followed it, through fields, a valley with a lake, large wood (two roe-deer, just yards away). Autumn was now starting in earnest, scuffed happily through piles of leaves.

Towards the end of the wood loggers had blocked the track – trees felled across it every 25m, in some cases dragged from elsewhere; it must have been deliberate. Château (closed) and abbey. Then 4km of that dead-straight road so dispiriting for walkers. Is that a building on the horizon, at the top of the slight rise, the edge of town? Don't look again in case it isn't. I'll die of boredom if my feet don't drop off first. Kept head up to be looked at, it's less scary for locals than skulking, turning away, blowing my nose just as they pass. But one attraction of this walk must be the fleeting, ephemeral nature of the human contacts. After all, a sedentary life may bring depth and richness – you learn in which part of the sky clouds will first appear, which tree will give the earliest plums, which neighbours can be trusted with which secrets, but it lacks drama and surprise. You don't get chatted up by a lady waiting to cross the road between the HGVs. You don't hear the young waitress rebuked by the manager for not cooling the cider (I'd asked for it as it was, and felt the bottle to check – you get more taste if it's room temperature). The look she gave him made it perfectly clear he was a disciplinarian fuss-pot, and probably a bottom-pincher too. One second that must enrich appreciation of the others. No chiffchaffs singing today, the first such; but woodlarks carolling away.

So into Noyant. Elegant, two-storey, white stone eighteenth century houses were laid out in straight roads and circuses. Was it my imagination to see in these small provincial towns a high proportion of drunk old men and mad people? And where was all this collecting of factual detail getting me? Was I just gathering impressions to see me through the dark? It was all part of the truth of France, but could it build up into a picture? Can't tell without trying, but was it distracting me from noticing more important things – about me, about the world, about others?

I stopped fretting as my spirits were suddenly lifted by a sense of the Midi in the late afternoon sunlight, the chestnuts, the vines, the figs. Ah! Just round the corner….. **16km**

Day 32: My target (the Loire) was now well within range. Another cold grey day with dull north-east wind. Autumn loomed. The bracken was colouring up, a dark purply copper, asparagus was changing from feathery green to fairy gold with red berries. Donkey as companion for a single stallion, aha! Banana trees, but no fruit. Two red squirrels.

At La Pellerine, the GR 36 rambled in from a long loop west, and out again on a long loop east. No accommodation in that direction, the one hotel being shut today, so I pressed on southwards. Ankle fine, so my hip was playing up. A white truck behind a barn, labelled 'Alpha Bulk Powders Ltd.', was the first sign of the UK for days, then six GB cars passed within 6km. What was going on? Later I learnt that there was a colony of Brits nearby, with holiday homes to let. Hip nagged for a few miles, then stopped as my ankle started to hurt quite sharply. I shambled along with a gait designed to appease ankle, hip, toenails, and blisters simultaneously (and failing to). A church tower showed up about 2km away – I hoped it was Vernoil, and not some intermediate hamlet. Another kilometre, and it had disappeared. Up a slight rise and there it was again, but no nearer. A second or third kilometre, and it suddenly took its place among a huddle of greyish-cream stone houses with slate roofs. I staggered into a bar where they were playing darts – a rarity in France, then phoned the hotel at La Breille-les-Pins. No problem for room or breakfast, but in theory they were on holiday until tomorrow, so no evening meal tonight, and I must arrive before 4.30pm. I gave up the chance of a win at darts and, despite the ankle, pressed on through extensive chestnut and pine woods, under an increasingly louring sky. Chestnut trees are another obsolescent technology. The wood is still used for its qualities of resistance to sun and water, but no-one subsists on the nuts, as whole areas of the Limousin, Corsica, and Northern Italy used to. Tennyson's

And only thro' the faded leaf
The chestnut pattering to the ground

was here a soft thunder of hundreds of thousands of spiky furry balls all falling. They lay disregarded on the forest floor. A maize-cage, with cobs. M Brou, only 40km away, had never heard of them – somewhere

I'd crossed yet another mini-frontier. Later I discovered this may have been a misunderstanding. People call them *séchoirs* – driers – but I see from a label that the manufacturers refer to them as *cribs*.

I left the hotel for a tour of the village, and returned two minutes later, laughing – no shops, no bar, no people, that was it! Mme Gaborit asked if I knew *la boule de fort*, the local variety of bowls. I'd never heard of it and five minutes later M Gaborit was taking me to the local club, a long anonymous shed only 50m away that I'd not paid any attention to. Inside was a bar with twenty-five people drinking. So that was where everyone was. Several left their drinks to put on a demonstration of the game for me, then invited me to play a couple of ends (I managed not to disgrace myself), while others practised more spectacular shots.

Many areas of France have their own sports. In parts of the Midi you can see nautical jousting (there are at least three forms of this); two forms of bull-fighting; tambourin – five-a-side tennis with a tambourine racket, the server has one on a stick, like a bed-warmer. *Pelote basque* is well-known, and most visitors to France will have noticed *pétanque* – men hurling metal bowls through the air. There are also *boule provençale* and *boule lyonnaise*. But *boule de fort* is played along the Loire between Angers and Tours, indoors and out. Every village hereabouts has one or more clubs. There are leagues for men's teams, women's teams, mixed teams, parent-and-child teams. The rink is flat, about 30m long, with gently curved-up sides. The bowls are flattened spheres of wood or plastic, aluminium-bound, with a slight bias. You can combine the bias with the curved sides of the rink to give the bowl an extraordinary zigzag trajectory. It was explained to me that the game originated among English sailors on wherries prevented from advancing up the Loire by lack of wind. In return I explained something of the basics of lawn (and crown-green) bowls. We adjourned to the bar for a *vin rosé*. I found myself talking to the Director of the Centre de Handicapés in the village, and an HGV driver who took apples all over UK. It's all eating apples, no cider, south of Le Mans. Impressive bellies clad in blue preceded men with hands like gloves full of concrete. Then back to the hotel, where M Gaborit stood us another glass of local *rosé*. We discussed whether the producer was the cousin or the son-in-law of someone in the bar. The most senior present, probably put up to it by the others, asked me if I was on my own (this is much trickier to ask in French, where *seul*, as well as 'on one's own' means 'alone' and 'lonely'; not quite 'single' but no wedding-ring may help the confusion). They roared approvingly when I explained that my wife was still at work, while I was retired and so free to ramble. My rather diffident explanations of what I was doing, and why, met everywhere with approval. 'Oh no, it's not crazy or stupid! I hope I can/wish I could do the same'. Nobody said or implied 'Do you blame your parents/wife/children?' or other such fashionable excuses for one's life. Mme Gaborit offered me a salad in my room – much better that a tin of mackerel, my alternative. It turned out to be a *salade composée* of six ingredients, with home-baked rolls, two sorts of cheese, a dessert … M Gaborit is an enthusiastic chef and gardener, and it showed. Must come back with Huguette some time (fourth such place, so far). **21km**

Day 33: Over breakfast, discovered why the hotel was new, a rarity among small French hotels, (though more than half of French houses have been built since 1945). The old one burned down in the 1980s killing the four people inside. A real disaster in a place as small and tightly knit as this. The new school across the road had its canteen closed last year – too few pupils, but they had managed to get the catering done by the Centre de Handicapés, and now kids were clamouring to get in. Set off in a dampish mist, no views over the Loire valley, as I had hoped. No vines either, but fields of tobacco, and drying sheds, and still lots of singing woodlarks. Greenwich Meridian for the seventh and penultimate time (though here it was not marked). Woman pumping water in her yard so vigorously that you could hear the clanks 100m away. Biggest log-pile yet – two rows of 1m30 logs, 2m50 high, over 200m long. Usual entry to French town – new roads at baffling angles, 'improvements' that always mean that it's pedestrians who have further to go. HGVs everywhere except on the motorway. Three kilometres of nasty, and three kilometres of merely disagreeable, road into town. Saumur is twinned with Warwick, perhaps because both are dominated by huge castles. Here, on 19 June 1940, when the

Germans had taken Paris, and all the Channel coast, and were accelerating across a demoralised France, when Pétain was begging Hitler for an armistice, there took place what Alistair Horne describes as 'one episode (that) ... will always leap forth from French history books in a blaze of glory ... Bock's Panzers ... reached Saumur on the Loire, the site of the famous cavalry school. Though still under instruction, the young cadets decided that they would not allow the school to fall without a fight. Armed only with training weapons, they held the Saumur bridges for two whole days against Panzers, until at last their ammunition ran out.'

As Macaulay wrote of the heroic defence of another bridge, that into Rome, by Horatius against the Etruscans:

Even the ranks of Tuscany
Could scarce forbear to cheer.

I arrived at the station. Time for a beer and a plate of delicious fresh chips – light, dry, crisp – then, with only 1000km still to go, took the train to Paris and winter quarters. **18km**

5

April – Saumur to Périgueux

Nearly a year ago I had ruled out spring walking, because of the uncertain weather, and out-of-season accommodation. So here I was, embarking on the next section on April 1. All along, I found myself expecting, and all along these expectations weren't met, not so much cheated as derailed. I started listing them. Perhaps in this way I could do two journeys simultaneously, one real, one imaginary; one given, one taken. I would hurry through muddy vineyards in a dark drizzle, arrive late at a dodgy hotel, see no interesting birds, horseshoes, donkeys, meet zero inhabitants. Or perhaps it would be glorious April weather, I'd stride out through lark-exalted fields, with spring in my step, to pass the time of day with gnarled *vignerons* tending their gnarled vines. Luckily, healthy reality gives what it gives, and I would take it.

Although France has long had the reputation of having the most centralised administration in Western Europe, everywhere you come across local variety, and pride in it. *Spécialités régionales* are a very obvious example, towns and villages have their own thing and are known for it. *Nougat de Montélimar, pruneaux d'Agen, calissons d'Aix, petits pâtés de Pézenas, bergamotes de Nancy, rillettes du Mans* and dozens of others are known and appreciated. They make acceptable gifts for travellers to bring home. It would be silly to write this off as mere hypocrisy – 'you could make these things anywhere' – or thoughtlessness; or to expect three or four centuries to have eliminated it, when opposed to the immutable forces of climate and geography, and the emotional power of inertia and local pride. France remains a country of inner frontiers.

There are *pays*, ill-defined areas such as Tarentaise, Puisaye, Caux, Lauragais, often giving their names to a number of villages or towns – St Valéry-en-Caux (and half a dozen others), Roissy-en-Brie (and at least thirty-two more). Then there are the provinces, the administrative districts from before the Revolution, many of which were independent before being acquired by the Crown – Brittany, Artois, Languedoc, Dauphiné, Alsace etc. These have no official existence today but all the French know in which province they live and were born.

The provinces were succeeded in 1790 by départements, of roughly equal size. The original scheme, typically French in its insistence on logic rather than common sense, was that they should be equal-sized squares, about eighty kilometres on each side, but luckily saner counsel prevailed. Originally eighty-three, there are ninety-five in metropolitan France. They all have geographical names (Landes, Jura, Haute-Saône etc) and are identified in post-codes, phone numbers, car-registration plates. Of course, the French know very well in which department they live, but there is no sentimental attachment. They say '*Je suis Lorrain*', or '*Provençale*', rather than '*Meurthe-et-Mosellan*' or '*Varoise*'.

The departments are grouped in various ways for educational, judicial or military purposes, and for the more modern administrative areas, into twenty-two *régions*. These have names that recall the old provinces (Languedoc-Roussillon, Picardie, Provence) or that are geographically descriptive (Midi-Pyrénées, Centre, Pays de la Loire). They, like the departments, have elected councils, with members of considerable political clout. When these are added to all the climatic, geographical, linguistic, historical and sociological frontiers, you can see that travelling in France, you're constantly crossing some more or less obvious frontier. The Loire, though not here separating administrations, is a whole bundle of these. North of the river, butter is the cooking fat, families are small and nuclear, parents and married children don't cohabit, unmarried and old people live on their own, there are fewer mid-wives, the weather is colder and wetter, fewer girls go to university, there is more insanity, more alcoholism, more suicide. To the south, cooking is done with oil, families are more patriarchal and extended, people are born and die at home, there is less alcoholism despite the quasi-totality of wine-production, more girls go on to higher education, the weather is warmer and drier. All this by and large, of course. In 1944 the Allies did not cross the Loire – the whole of south-western France between the Loire and the Rhone liberated itself.

Day 34: Leaving Saumur station, and stopping only to remember the heroic cadets of 1940, I crossed this magic water by the Pont des Cadets into the town of Saumur. And it was market day. Markets are *la France profonde* in all her multicoloured splendour. Some are permanent, some weekly, some specialised, eg in shoes, junk, philately, most are general. Not all products are local, since stalls take the place of a village shop. Sometimes you see a North African stall, with *harissa* (the hot pepper paste to go with couscous), plates with bright geometrical patterns,

Market day

brass, cloth. All are selling things you won't find elsewhere – pigs' trotters in parsley, head-cheese, rocket, six kinds of bean, live rabbits and quail, seedlings of leeks and brassicas, unpasteurised cheese (labelled as such). The plastic basket you collect your vegetables in is reweighed for each item. And the weighing machines! In Ajaccio market, in 1980, I saw goods weighed on the *romaine*, the 4000-year-old arm balance. On visits in the 1990s, though, there was only one in (furtive) use. Would you like your cheese *habité* (lived in) they asked. Maggots are a delicacy to some. Fat women in urban France have to write off to mail-order firms to get supplies of underwear, but in the street-markets of *la France profonde*, knickers up to size 56 are traded openly across the stall counter.

Behind the overbearing château on the limestone plateau, every village was dominated by vines, or estates of huge warehouses with sightless walls and roofs, brightened only by huge agribusiness slogans: *ENGRAIS DE L'OUEST*, or BOOTS HEALTHCARE (!), and those acronyms beloved by the French, that make Brits giggle: *SODEXHO, FRANPOM, SODEMA*. Although Saumur is home to the National Riding School and the château houses the Museum of the Horse, there were hardly any horses about from now on, certainly nothing like the ubiquitous trotters of the Orne.

I had a beer in the bar in Brézé; it was the wrong thing, as everyone was drinking white wine as an *apéro.* All who came in shook hands, even with me, an obvious, beer-drinking, stranger. Back-streets in one village were *ruettes*, a dialect word, here elevated to official status. The local limestone, *tuffeau*, is excellent building material. Easy to quarry, it hardens on exposure to air. And it makes good caves, too. Some, up the Loire, are still lived in, though round here they're mushroom farms, stores, garages, barns etc. I spotted a sea-urchin fossil staring up at me from the gutter, and collected it for Huguette. Although a jay's blue wing-feather is what I usually try to get her, spring isn't moulting time. A few *vignerons* were out toiling among the vines, 400 yards from each other. It's a lonely working life until the harvest.

Not far away to the east was the Abbaye de Fontevraud, a huge group of mediaeval ecclesiastical buildings. The chapel contains the tombs of the English Plantagenet kings – Henry II, Richard the

Lionheart. Shouldn't we ask for them back? When I hitched through here in 1956 it was still being used as a prison, but we were shown round by the parish priest, who'd given us a lift from Saumur. Now it's a real tourist high point. Go.

Like a wave under a carpet, spring was driving north, pushing up first violets, daffodils and dog's mercury, then cowslips and primroses, now ladies' smock. Into Montreuil-Bellay, with a château built (1025) by Fulk Nerra (Fulk the Black, to distinguish him from his ancestors Fulk the Red and Fulk the Good), an archetypal mediaeval baron of these parts. On the cemetery wall was a plaque to two men shot by the Germans at 11.30pm on August 24, 1944. As only too often, their names and ages were all one learned about them; the circumstances of the killings are not given. If there is a book describing all these monuments, of which there must be thousands, and giving more details, I have yet to find it. The Americans had reached the Loire, 25km away ten days before, and Paris was liberated the very next day, but the Germans were still executing hostages right up to the last minute.

I was offered a glass of the local bubbly in the hotel bar, by a young man who turned out to be the hotel's owner. A *vigneron* came in, but he wasn't the maker of our wine, and the job had made him taciturn. Neither knew anything about the plaque on the cemetery wall; conversation languished. **22km**

Day 35: The most expensive breakfast yet, at £4.50, 6.50 euros, but good value, since it included ham, eggs, cheese. My pattern was to eat very little at midday, so I filled up now. It was the shooting close season, and everyone was out fishing (it was the close fishing season in the UK, strangely enough). At one little lake, several techniques were in evidence; feather floats near the bank, chubbier ones further out, ledgers, spinners, banks of five rods with no-one in attendance. One fisherwoman. Picnicking families. It turned out there had been a *lâcher de truites*, several hundred trout released, yesterday, to provide the weekend's sport. The village bar, where I learned this, was also plastered with jokes such as 'with age, stiffness merely changes place'. Oh! Ho! Ho! Across huge empty fields, with only one or two farms (deserted). A single tree, visible of course, for miles, had attracted the waymarkers. Later they lost me twice; the second time I found myself three metres up in the air astride a fence in the middle of a heronry. What on earth was I doing here? Valiantly, I fought my way out of the undergrowth and back onto the GR. I was moving steadily away from blue sky towards purple, though the rain managed to hold off, along the banks of the Thouet, which were increasingly lined with small shacks for weekend and summer use. Some were in brick or stone, and some in carefully shaped planking, but some were mere allotment huts; there were two lorry trailers, caravans, a container, a railway truck ... All were closed. Birds were everywhere, but non-avian wildlife was restricted to few butterflies, and a solitary frog, pop-eyed in expectation of a gorgeous goggling partner.

Into Thouars (twinned with Helensburgh, I'm told, though I saw no sign) along the towpath. The cabins were now shoulder-to-shoulder; downstream, surprisingly, of the outfall of the Water Purification Works. The GR here is one of the mediaeval pilgrims' routes to Compostela. There was even a street-sign 'rue de Compostelle' at one point. My stick started causing confusion again. Under a railway bridge was a plaque to the vice-mayor, who, in 1947, when it was under reconstruction, saw a fire threatening to undo all the work, and walked out on the bridge in the night. It was too late: bridge and he fell into the river.

I crossed yet another mini-frontier somewhere today. Telephone numbers now no longer started with 02, but with 05. The riverside and town-centre were full of typical family groups, two or three generations out for a post-gigantic-lunch walk. A funfair in the town square had attracted hundreds. Telephone kiosk that admitted wheelchairs.

Very friendly *chambre d'hôte* in town (the two local hotels are closed on Sunday evenings!). Both *Monsieur* and *Madame* were doctors, she in charge of hospital radiology units in the north of the department. Why did they take paying guests? For the conversation, it appeared. I was invited to an *apéritif* and chat with friends, and did my best to be informative about the NHS, witty about holidays in Tunisia, interesting about the other topics that were raised. The NHS has a terrible press in France. You can hardly open a newspaper without reading some unfavourable (and often incorrect) comment on it. There are French people who won't visit the UK in case they fall ill or have an accident. **24km**

Day 36: Rain on the shutters woke me. After an excellent and sociable breakfast with hosts who could not understand that I like walking on my own (reasons not to walk in a group: you never all walk at the same rhythm, stop at the same time for the same reasons, complain about the same things), I lost my way in the town, but then found good waymarks, some even giving times and distances, along the river. There is no topoguide in print for the GR 36 between Le Mans and Angoulême, but waymarks and the ordinary maps, are quite sufficient. Through rained-on fields and woods where only a streakiness announced summer's green, in a slight daze. Was the ibuprofen I was taking to avoid recurrence of the hip-problem having mental effects? Sometimes I seemed to be having intermittences, if not of consciousness, then certainly of attention. Past giant bird-farm, at least 1km square in which tens of thousands of pheasants were being bred for a shooting *lâcher*. The *café* in St Généroux was in uproar. More than fifty men in tens and half-dozens were eating in three very small rooms. Three waitresses scurried round in semi-controlled panic. My entrance in dripping cape, and with staff, caused hardly a blink. There was a notice behind the bar for Marion, aged ten, who disappeared from her home in Agen in November 1996, causing a national uproar. Her picture is still shown in small bars – I saw at least four others – many miles from Agen. But there's never been any news.

Grill (lamb steaks and ham, on wood fire) smelled delicious. I was served my beer slowly, as the workers had to be got away before two, supposedly, but I was happy simply to dry off. At 2.30pm the main group was still singing:

Il est vraiment,
Il est vraiment,
Il est vraiment phénoménal
(cp For he's a jolly good fellow).

All these (the conviviality, the appreciation of children, even the singing) are links that, consciously or not, bind French society together, and of which any outsider who wants to understand them, must take cognizance.

It is the secret sympathy,
The silver link, the silken tie,
Which heart to heart, and mind to mind,
In body and in soul can bind.

Though Scott of course was talking about true love, not social bonds. (Note on reading matter for solitary walkers: I took Shakespeare's *Sonnets* for the first stage – not a success, too concentrated for a tired pedestrian. In October I took *In Memoriam*; that was much better, with an unbeatable blend of continuity and self-containedness. You could read three sections one evening, and pick up the thread the next day with no difficulty. This time I had Scott – not a success either. Too long, too diffuse, and the narrative far too hidden; sometimes I wondered if he could follow it himself. It was the heaviest, too. Next time?)

In the afternoon, a stoat crossed the track behind me; a water-rat swam straight at me, then hurriedly away. I failed to find the *gîte* I had booked for this evening. It was sign-posted over a mile away, but when I got there, the building wasn't marked at all. After trudging up and down in the rain for miles, peering at houses and barns, I went to the town to find a phone, and discovered there were two cheap but acceptable hotels not mentioned in the tourist list. Thoroughly fed up by now, I booked in. Spent an instructive hour in the bar with the local paper.

The *Comité des Fêtes* (Entertainments Committee) of the next village, Gourgé, was organising *La Transgourgéenne*, circuits round the village. You pay, get coffee and croissants, set off on one of three circuits – 25km, 30km, 50km. What! Oh, that's for cyclists. The walk is 15km, and you get a sandwich and drink at finish. All for £2, 3 euros.

Old weather-saying for today was 'On April 3, the cuckoo sings alive or dead'. Very gnomic, I'm sure. Surely journalists simply make these up?

Priceless example of French grammar: '*Le mannequin français, Laetitia Casta, a-t-il choisi de vivre à Londres pour échapper à l'impôt'*. ('Has the French model LC chosen to live in London to avoid taxes?') What's so odd is lost in translation, I'm afraid. But since the word *mannequin* is masculine, all grammatical agreements must be masculine. So *français, il,* even though they refer to a girl. Mlle Casta herself is the model for the busts of Marianne (cp Britannia) now being installed in every

French town hall. (In fact, she'd chosen to live in London to be with her boyfriend.) They take pride in sticking to these anti-common-sense rules, too. There's a very wide gap in French between the word and the thing it refers to. French often seems to have little possibility for poetry. Not for them the aural symbolism beloved by English-speakers, whereby words like *squelch, peep, wheedle* seem to contain something of their meaning; where *jelly, welly, belly* share a semantic component, as do *bash, crash, dash, flash, slash, smash, thrash* etc. But not *cache, sache*, and especially not *vache*.

The hotel catered for travelling reps, all single men. I've seen this before, and know the drill. You mustn't sit directly facing each other. Back-to-back, back-to-front, sideways-on are OK. You can talk. And breakfast starts an hour earlier than most hotels, at 6.45am. **28km**

Day 37: Anxious moment after breakfast when my credit card failed to pass the machine. Luckily only this once and I'd enough cash. It rained all the morning. I'd trouble with the map, too. St Loup-Lamairé turned out to be St Loup-sur-Thouet; Lamairé is 5km away. Oiron, a village with a potentially useful hotel, wasn't named on the map at all. Gourgé was spelled Courgé. Then there are problems with the French convention of leaving accents off capital letters, so that BREZE can have three different pronunciations (Brézé, Brèze, Brezé) and GOURGE two. Mrs Acland-Troyte, in her dog-cart, in 1886, falls into this trap (boom! boom!), referring consistently to 'Brèze' (it's Brézé). This makes asking the way a nightmare. And in addition to these, there's a tourist-board snobbery. Provinces are smarter than boring old departments, so Maine-et-Loire is referred to in their brochures and maps as Anjou (of which it's only part) and Dordogne as Périgord.

After 5km on road I found an attractive little variant of the GR 36, along the river. One problem with rain is where to sit down, where to consult the map. I stopped at picnic-site toilets - 'No gipsies. No travellers' - to check route. After that, keeping my footing on the mud occupied my whole attention, and I was soon lost. Trudged along road, through countryside much less interesting than I'd hoped, but very empty. My appearance caused great excitement among the livestock – snorting heifers jostled for attention, sheep gathered up their lambs and scarpered. Light drizzle that redoubled in intensity if I took my hood off. The landmark church of Gourgé, on top of a hill, came usefully into view. At a fine mediaeval bridge, in a hamlet of perhaps seven houses, a bulldozer and grab was demolishing a building. All the inhabitants had been drawn to the woeful sight of the roof being knocked in, floor-beams being dragged out and piled neatly nearby; debris that only a moment ago had been walls still serving a long useful purpose, was scraped up and dumped in a skip.

In the bar in Gourgé, white or *rosé* was still the *apéritif*; not yet the aniseed drinks of the south. But the barmaid did exclaim *'Ah putain, c'est vrai!'* in sudden dismay. And the roofs have started to look southern too – low, shallow pitch, tile, reddish-rose. Two or three men were assassinating the character of another inhabitant; a woman, I think a business rep, came in alone for a meal. Nobody commented on this – a revolution in itself.

Fountain at Parthenay

The weather cheered up while I was in the bar, and the landscape was no longer a uniform greyish-green, but full of lovely deep greens and purples; the narrow muddy paths of the morning had changed to spacious droves, stone-based, tree-lined, with only occasional patches of mud. They'd make ideal walking on a hot summer day, and I started making plans to come back and see them on one.

The path took a long and unnecessary ramble round Parthenay parks and river-banks where the water was polluted by agricultural fertiliser and slaughterhouse waste. Perhaps all those cabins clustered downstream from the Thouars Water

Purification Works were sensibly situated after all. The entry into the mediæval town was very impressive. And the modern town is neatly kept, too; there are fountains, of which the French are fond, whereas they tend to remind Brits simply of rain. I checked into a posh hotel, so as to get a bath – you can't coddle sore feet in a shower. In the restaurant, wives were keeping their husbands in order by choosing their own meal, then trying 'just a teeny bit' of his. Day's fauna – two frogs. **27km**

Day 38: Boring suburban exit from town, all slip-roads, hypermarkets, leylandii hedges. Then suddenly GR 364 plunged off, and within 1km came two surprises. First was a big church, thirteenth or fourteenth century, which must have held several hundreds, now deconsecrated and disused, with only pigeons inside. No steps, just turf right up to the open door. Second was an old stone bridge made of slabs, with concrete repairs, and clearly constructed by a miniature drunk, winding its way across some tiny rapids. Then glorious mud, where the stick came in handy for support, as both my feet were halfway up the bank. I emerged eventually on to a dual carriageway; a kingfisher flashed across. I followed by-roads, where the farm dogs were quite nasty. One, in particular, followed me growling and snapping, despite being shouted at and threatened. Picking up a stone worked wonders, though – I'd no sooner bent down than the beast was fifty metres away. I walked with my stick at trail, to protect my ankles, in case it returned. And, as if to demonstrate how dangerous dogs can be for vehicles as well as walkers, another beast ran out at me, only a few kilometres further on, right into track of a motorcyclist. He swerved, braked, recovered, cursed, sped off. The dog's owner called it back in before it could wreak further havoc.

I was looking at the map in St Pardoux when the school transport arrived. The driver caught my eye and looked away, but two children, aged thirteen to fourteen asked if I was looking for something. Polite, friendly, un-nosy, they gave clear and correct directions, and said that if I followed them through the village, it would be even easier. It was. Thank you.

My spirits lifted, I plodded miles in the rain to Mazières. It had no bypass, huge HGVs trundled constantly up the main street, old ladies waited five minutes in the rain to cross to the shops and five minutes to get back home. The bar served food, so I warmed up. Others eating were two young women at one table, and at the other, four local workmen discussing people they'd known since childhood, in harmless high spirits. They broke into choruses of *Tant qu'elle est rousse* – So long as she's a redhead – and pretended they'd forgotten their wallets. Two girls known to them came in and got good-humouredly ragged. The two strangers at the other table were wholly uncommented-on. They didn't moderate their language for either pair – *merde, connard, branleur, tête de con, bordel, putain;* all better left untranslated, especially literally. Their mobile rang, it was the boss wondering where on earth they'd got to; giggling, they claimed to be on their way, and left. The mixture of traditional (the joshing, the language, the high spirits) and a little modernity (the mobile) is typical. Change is something the French are very wary of. Sometimes it can usefully be blamed on foreigners. Laws imposed by Europe to prevent the shooting of migrating birds, McDonalds, globalisation, are resented, in some quarters bitterly. Changes that can be blamed on the government, such as those to make tax-paying easier, also have their enemies. But those that come from within – the disappearance of village shops, small petrol-stations, hotels, bars or the terrifying increase in road-freight, are hardly opposed. Of course it's harder to find a scapegoat.

Rain every step of the afternoon. I passed two rabbits and four donkeys, all of us drenched. Over to the east was Melle, with the silver-mines of early kings of France (fifth to tenth centuries). This was the Seuil du Poitou, between the extremity of Armorican granite somewhere near Mazières, and the Massif Central. This threshold allowed communication between Aquitaine and the Loire Valley. This was the corridor which the Arab army swept through in 732, before being defeated by Charles Martel near Tours, and driven back to Spain. Its gradual control by the French crown, in the Hundred Years War, was the beginning of the end for the English, split into Aquitaine and Normandy.

Cold and dispirited, I arrived at the *chambre d'hôte.* It was empty except for an unfriendly dog. I sheltered in freezing barn for forty-five minutes before Madame arrived and showed me to huge chilly room. Unlike the over-cosiness of Normandy, south of the Loire, the rooms tend to be modest in furnishings, spartan even. But first impressions were misleading again; several other people were staying, and the evening meal was a success – excellent food, too. Conversation ran from advertising, to golf, local tourist attractions, property prices, Paris restaurants (recommendation to visit the Tour d'Argent for its duck – as unnecessary a piece of advice as I can remember, the duck is world famous anyway, and well above my pocket). There was an agreeable difference between the young people (well, about thirty) and a middle-aged businessman, who couldn't resist comparing France and the UK. The fact that the UK drives on the left is a source of ill-concealed irritation to many French people. 'Why don't you drive on the right like everybody else?' I've tried several counters, from the factual, 'a third of the world's population drives on the left', via the reasonable, 'what would be the advantage? And think of the cost of changing' and the persuasive, 'it's the *exception culturelle* – you can listen to Johnny Halliday, and we can drive on the left', to the counter-attack, 'do you like being like everybody else?' You could also ask why French trains drive on the left. While the others simply got on talking, and comparisons were incidental, his generation still needs to justify itself *vis-à-vis* the British, the difference is the subject of conversation. Though many of his comparisons were fair, even favourable to the UK, it's a limitation. **25km**

Day 39: Breakfast with the least talkative of last night's guests, a shy girl, whose face, rather stolid in repose, turned out to be charming in animation. She was training people at the nearby chemical factory to use the instruments (spectrometers etc) that her firm had sold them. She travelled all over France, and, though less, in North Africa. Looked barely twenty-two – I really must be ageing! I'll be making an effort not to address them as 'dear' next; and then not even bothering to make the effort. I travelled white roads and some GR to Niort where the roadside banks were carpeted with spring flowers – cowslips, which the French confusingly call *coucous* like the birds, anemones, orchids and some big purple flowers that cluster flat on the ground, with no apparent stem or leaves. What are these? I started to pass trees destroyed in the December storms, when France lost millions of trees. Some were uprooted because of their situation, to leeward of roads, rivers, ditches, for instance, which meant they had no roots on the side that needed them, and many were simply snapped off one or five metres up. It was a truly appalling sight – they were laid out in rows like earthquake or massacre victims, in a fearful symmetry. I started to have serious doubts about the two days woodland walking south of Niort. But laying off the ibuprofen had been the right thing, I was feeling much more alert.

In one village a farm still bore plaques celebrating prizes won at cattle shows in the 1920s. The local breed, the Parthenay, is known for its qualities as a meat- and milk-giver, but is famous for its butter. At one point, the path headed for a crane, which turned out to be on a motorway under construction. All was fenced off, the footbridge hardly started, but someone had carefully separated the barbed-wire strands that crossed the path, so I climbed through too, down a mud slope, across the carriageways, nodding to chaps in hard hats, up the other side and away. Curious five-barred gates, several over a distance of 5m. The hinge-post was 3-4m high, held by two cast-iron hoops set in neighbouring tree or even concrete post. A long diagonal bar from top to far bottom. Sometimes the hoops remained though the gate had long gone. I was nearly bowled over by a snorting jogger barging along the verge.

A shortish day, so an early arrival in Niort, up a long street between institutional walls and some unimaginative graffiti. This is much more widespread than in England, though it is a similar melange of the rude, the crude, the witty, the decorative. In France graffiti have a long history and a semi-official status; some trend-setters would like to make them an art-form. In a country where nobody puts election posters in the window for fear of a brick or a vendetta, they are the only anonymous form of public expression. The Tour de France has special road-men who travel ahead of the cyclists on the next day's route, putting the names across the tarmac. It looks very strange to see SEAN YATES written across the top of a minor Pyrenean mountain-pass. And then there are the political ones: *ALGERIE FRANCAISE* from 1960; *NON A L'AUTOROUTE* at various times and places;

Graffiti on a railway bridge in Sète

GARDAREM LOU LARZAC from the early seventies; *NON* (or *OUI) A DE GAULLE* from 1968; *LIBEREZ* _____ , almost constantly. Among the few English equivalents are MARPLES MUST GO on the early M 1 bridges and the more recent SEND CRUISE BACK. But surprisingly, English is the international language of graffiti as of so much else: PLEASE WASH ME appears on dusty cars in provincial Mexico, as well as WANK PORNO (whatever can they make of that?). The oldest I know is *VIVE DORIOT PPF A BAS STALINE* on a railway bridge in Sète. Jacques Doriot was a French National Socialist leader of the 1930s, who collaborated with the Nazis, and was killed in 1945. I don't know that some aged follower doesn't creep out with a paint-pot to refresh it, but it was still legible in 2000.

That evening in the bar I listened to a small girl reciting her homework to her mother. Later in a Tunisian restaurant I eavesdropped shamelessly on three people engaged in heated, and technical, conversation about the French Higher Education system as regards research and its funding. With my mind still on language, I couldn't help being annoyed at their use of 'Anglo-Saxon', as though New Zealanders, Scots, Kansans were alike in their systems, and the French standing alone against it. Retaliate by referring to them as 'Latino-Belges'. **20km**

Day 40: Sky cloudless, but cold. I took advantage of the rainlessness to sit down by the roadside after leaving Niort, at last just sitting. In between the shrill whines of lorries passing on the motorway I could hear the rustle of the cereal leaves, now a good foot long. A roller-blader passed. Like yesterday's jogger, he was timing himself, said nothing, wore a Walkman. As with mobile phones, these are designed to cut you off from physical surroundings (aural and social ones at least). Why don't these chaps just lie on the bedroom floor and wave their legs about? Artisans zipped nimbly by in neat little vans. Car-drivers raced along, pulling up only for piss-stops. Speeding is a national sport, only just ahead of that of being over the alcohol limit when you do it. Ninety people were killed on the roads at the Easter weekend this year, and ninety-two the weekend after. Only Portugal and Greece, with much older cars, far worse roads and inferior hospital facilities, exceed the annual French road-deaths figure of 8000 (proportionately to their population, of course). The French take great, mainly justified, pride in being in control of a vehicle, in knowing its limits and possibilities. Just bad luck on those who aren't, and on those who can't see round corners. Excuses are legion: 'They're suicides, at heart', 'It's our Latin temperament,' – point out that the Italians, those *nec-plus-ultra* Latins, have fewer road-deaths. I've not yet heard 'It's our tradition, you see.'

A cold wind meant I walked fully buttoned-up despite brilliant sunshine. Through villages with more names on the war memorial than on the electoral roll to a small bar, where the barman, Dédé, had no sense of people at all. I sat down, parked my sack and stick. Had I broken down on the motorway, he asked. I explained all, stood him a drink – *pastis* here, at last – we chatted about changes in village life. When I asked the way on leaving, he indicated what would be a simple route for a motorist. I saved several kilometres by finding quite acceptable minor roads, full of motorists as it happened. Crossed small stream, the bottom of which was crawling with caddis-fly larvae. *Chambre d'hôte* was cheap and comfortable, unlike the village restaurant which was pretentious, over-priced and served rather small quantities. I'd have done better to choose the 'greasy spoon' opposite . **22km**

Day 41: Disagreeable dreams, dissipated by rational daylight. France is not a superstitious country, though many of its inhabitants are. On the French-Swiss frontier I once saw a bat zoom past me in a midnight flash of lightning. In the Black Forest, or perhaps Scotland, not to mention Transylvania, that would have struck a lasting terror. But not there, nor here. A keen spring light, young and merciless, beat on my head – the first sweating day. Raimbault was a village of friendly dogs; many just looked, two followed me inside their fence, grimacing, two chased after me out of the village, pretending I was taking them for a walk. Their owner recalled them by ultrasonic whistle. The path here was called the Tour de la Sylve d'Argençon. What images the name calls up – a romantic local beauty, woodland glades, a heroine of Nerval, a rustle of silvery leaves, a dryad. But the forest had been badly battered in the winter gale. In some areas nothing remained standing, just desolation and wood piles. What were they going to do with it all? I'd intended to walk straight through the forest of Chizé, but this part turned out to be fenced off – it's the Biological Sciences Study Centre of the National Hunting Bureau, so a wildlife reserve. It needed a three-kilometre detour, then a long walk beside the fence. But, of course, remarkable wildlife. Two migrating White Storks on their way, perhaps, to the valley of the Risle, some Brent Geese, a Goshawk, roe-deer. A green lizard in the wood, scaly, pointy, broad-headed, greeny-gold; and butterflies – Peacock, Brimstone, Skipper, Clouded Yellow, Red Admiral, and many I don't know. The track deteriorated from metalled road to stone, from stone to mud, then became frankly an overgrown ditch, but was still waymarked with occasional old milestones saying 11.45, 11.38, 11.25. Could make no sense of this before they too disappeared. Then for 1km had to fight my way through, round, over, under fallen trees; zig-zag is a euphemism. This took hours and compelled a change of route for the next four days.

I lost my way before arriving in Aulnay, which has a very fine church, St Pierre, all of a piece, shown on the cover of the IGN map Niort-Angoulême. It has been described by Kingsley Amis, never at his best in francophobe mode, as 'an unaccoutred frowsty barn', but looked fine to me. In the town I found nobody had heard of a hotel, even 400 yds away; it was closed, and shuttered; no, it wasn't, the door opened when I knocked, and it was really quite welcoming. I chatted with Madame in the bar (she stood me a beer). 'My husband's cooking the meal,' she said. 'He loves doing that.' They were trying to sell up, but couldn't get the price they wanted despite some young couples being quite interested. She had hard things to say about *chambres d'hôte* taking hotel business away. They'd had various real pilgrims through, English, Dutch, Australians, Canadians, on the way to Compostela, some even with cards to be stamped for authentication. In the town, the stones gave out the day's stored heat, men played *pétanque*, the church glowed in the evening light, lilac flowered, a Crested Lark picked crumbs outside the telephone box. **29km**

Day 42: The GR now has four days through woodland, but after yesterday's slow progress, I had to avoid that. So short-cut south on minor roads. More uninteresting countryside. Endless fields of grass and mud. Rain was falling, bored and non-committal, as if it simply couldn't think of anything better to do. Temporary electricity and telephone wires still drooping along hedges (they were all blown down by the gale). I approached one village zig-zagging like a siege engine, never frontally, finally arriving at the same time as a procession of cars. Funeral? Wedding? No black or white ribbons, though, or honking. Seventy-five people got out, including children (one being carried), dogs (one ditto), leaders etc, and started walking round the village. The scene was further enlivened by a herd of cows being driven up the main street. A man with recording equipment stopped to interview me (and I him). It was the Charente-Maritime branch of a national association for village buildings – to sensitize everyone, including owners and inhabitants, to their architectural treasures. Here they consisted mainly of big seventeenth and eighteenth century farm buildings with impressive arched entrances to central courtyards. Disappointingly, I was less interesting than he thought, and explanation of my presence was unrecorded. But a rather nice atmosphere I thought, and I looked with fresh eyes at the next villages.

Rain all the way. At least, there was never a moment at which I could be certain that some drop wasn't winging its way towards me. Long trek across quiet fields full of buttercups radiating into space. At last

Matha. I plunged into first bar. There was a notice advertising DART'S CLUB – a prime example of *'épicier's apostrophe'* – as in Chez Maxim's, Le Coconut's Beach, Discothèque le Jack's, *un pin's*, Superdrug', even, though in Andorra, *Jack D'aniel's*. Or so I thought. In French, it's evidence of an anglophile snobbery, not simple illiteracy or carelessness, as in English. But here it was probably English influence. Two Englishmen at the counter were reading the *Daily Mail* and *The Times* and chatting up a suspiciously good-looking sixteen-year-old. Bar closed at 2pm. I went round the deserted town and was asked the way by a clearly desperate driver (not the only time this happened, despite my stick and rucksack). But there was a second bar with twenty kids playing pool, and one lonely Brit at the counter. (Why do Brits sit at the counter? They do it at home too, blocking everyone's access.) I bought postcards of donkeys. The French National Donkey Stud near here has been breeding back to the *baudet du Poitou*, the local mediaeval beast of burden. Postcards featuring these genetically reconstituted mokes went to my more irreverent friends. The bar music included *Reet petite, I've got you, babe, It's a rich man's world, If you go down to San Francisco, Guantanamera*; this was Chérie FM, but where were the French hits of yesteryear? What had happened to the *exception culturelle*?

Endless fields of grass and mud

I observed the kids. There were no (audible) comments on other groups, me, the Brit at the counter; no needle, no aggression, just lively innocuous conversation. There was some half-hearted attempt to muddle the barman as to what they'd eaten and drunk, but he knew them all personally, and they knew it. Older people drifted in after lunch, but there was no heaviness between older men and young girls. When two men went out to talk on the pavement, others shouted '*La porte*!' They closed it, it was not a problem, not an issue about who could/couldn't shout at whom, there was no face at stake, no misplaced pride. Older ones, seventeen to eighteen that is, particularly the girls, smoked; some drank cognac, some beer, most soft drinks. Getting drunk wasn't an issue, either.

Resumed towards the *chambre d'hôte*, and some peasant almost killed me. I was walking on the left, facing the traffic, so as to see as much as possible. A car was coming, close to the verge (I thought, later, that the driver was short-sightedly using the verge to navigate by) so held my stick in right hand as a marker. He/she went straight past, an inch from my arm, and some part of the car banged against the trailing end of my stick, I yelled, turned round, gesticulated. The car following him hooted and flashed, so he stopped, at a safe distance, to examine his bodywork. I was unhurt, so I went on walking. If he wanted to make something of it, he could turn round. Then we'd see. (He didn't.)

What nice people at the *chambre d'hôte*. Madame drove me in the rain to the village restaurant and arranged to be rung by the proprietor when I'd finished, so that she could pick me up. Which she did. Good meal, too. **27km**

Day 43: Rain all night and all this morning. Over breakfast I heard more about the December gale. Gusts of 135mph had been recorded in Matha. Eventually I set off on what promised to be the most boring day so far. It was. The villages were small, uninteresting, barless. It was a dog day too. A high proportion of France's fifteen million mutts barked at me. At one place at least six were yelping hysterically while their owner hung out of a window doing nothing to abate the racket. 'Doesn't this noise bother you?' I shouted. She couldn't hear me. Just who/what are these beasts 'protecting' by thus aggressing innocent passers-by? If their children made such a din they'd be in court in a trice. As well as being world champions of medication, and at the time of writing, of football, the French are probably world champions of paranoia. *L'insécurité* is a subject of anxious discussion, even in small villages where one chap stealing a chicken constitutes a crime-wave. Two thirds of them claim to have anxiety fits; twenty-one per cent get up at least once in the night to check that the front door is locked. How do I know this? Well, they're also world opinion-poll champions.

This was by far the least rambler-friendly part of France I'd crossed. One incident cheered me up. A middle-aged woman pruning her hanging baskets saw me coming up the road. Pausing only to aim her spaniel at me, she collected her gear and ran indoors, so that I'd have to climb the fence, disable her dog, and smash the patio doors if I wanted to ask for a glass of water. The dog barked half-heartedly, then heard the doors sliding-to behind him. He tried to get back in. She waved him at me, 'Go and bark at the man!' He pawed the door, whining, keener to get out of the rain. I passed, laughing. *'Bonjour Madame!'*

These were the *fins bois* vineyards of Cognac. Not for the top brandies (*grande champagne, fine champagne, borderies*, in descending order) but better than the mere *bons bois. Vignerons,* and one *vigneronne*, were pruning and tying-up, wearing big sacking pinafores with pockets for secateurs, string etc.

Today's drivers were almost all attentive to walkers, pulling across, signalling even, to give me room. Just one old, slow, two-peasant car, again meticulously tracking the verge, crawled past my elbow (still at lethal speed, be it said), the occupants raising eyebrows at the near miss. Clearly they'd expected me to leap fully-clothed into the ditch. More odd saints: Sainte Sévère (patron saint of masochists?), Saint Même (ditto). Two dead hedgehogs on the road set me thinking of imagination (how could they possibly imagine the dazzle, the speed, the weight?), its origins, its evolutionary use, how easy and how dangerous to let it control.

Jarnac, celebrated, round here anyway, as the birthplace of the former President François Mitterrand, didn't at all give the impression of a working town. Everyone moved very slowly, including me by now; there were no snappy businessmen with suits, and pouches under their arms (and eyes); the *café* was full of couples, kids, old mates of the barman. Many of the girls seemed to have curiously hard, shrunken, Jivaro, heads. Hotel was small, rather decrepit, expensive. I talked with the handyman in the bar, who appeared to be working free. We discussed the lighting, whether or not to rip out the cladding, what colour the ceiling should be. 'All my friends are gaga up at the home,' he said, 'and my family's all dead, so I just do what pleases me.' Generator hum kept me awake too much of the night. **26km**

Day 44: Grumpily insomniac, I spent the morning listing the faults of the French – their wonderful mixer-taps (*mitigeurs*), backed-up by hopeless waste-evacuation systems. The national shortage of places for putting things down – windowsills, soap-dishes, coat-hooks on the backs of WC doors. Their ability to have their cake and eat it, and their enthusiasm for doing so – Joan of Arc and World War II are examples that irritate all Brits. The way everything closes on Mondays. Their shooting blackbirds and thrushes to eat. Their appallingly slow, inefficient and obstructive administration (though to be fair they suffer this themselves). Their penchant for alfresco urinating. Their gullibility to any intellectual or cultural pretentiousness. Their strange diseases that no-one else has – *crises de foie, cellulite, spasmophilie* and their equally strange treatments – vitamized toothpaste, spas, salt-water therapy. Their way of insisting that French things are not simply preferable, or more familiar to them, but actually better. Etc, etc.

Purging myself of these images of a sleepless night, I left town past luxurious brandy châteaux, then along the Charente – upstream, of course – with broad, full, weighty swirls in the current, wondering at the single-mindedness of water. *Vignerons*. Fishermen. Old man with his dog. Then a solitary dog; nose down, he detoured round me, more interested in tracking the delicious smells of the old man's bitch. Storm-wreckage, whole trees, still going downstream. A pleasure-boat, from an English company in Jarnac, going up. A man was poling a punt upstream; Oxford end, I was glad to see. Then a string of pretty villages – St Simon *'village gabarrier'*. The *gabarres* were boats poled, sailed or rowed up the Charente, and other rivers without tow-paths, for the wine-trade. One workshop was recreating a *gabarre*; there was a tiny museum. Brassac had a splendid romanesque abbey, in clean, light yellow stone; a three-tier tower topped by a spire. I dawdled in the chapel feeling more like a pilgrim than ever. St Simeux had a neat church and a village grocery, signed two or three miles out. I bought provisions on principle. Somewhere about here I crossed the Greenwich Meridian for the eighth and last time, then sat on a wall by the river, watching raptors and an Orphean Warbler, till rain closed in again. I lost the GR (both possible tracks were blocked by fallen trees), but didn't try too hard, as the *topoguide* says that waymarks here are often destroyed. Why can't these unreconstructed peasants see that signs will get the ramblers off their land quicker than if they're lost and wandering helplessly about?

I arrived quite suddenly at the *chambre d'hôte*. Nice M and Mme Bouchard questioned me with friendly concern, and before I was fairly indoors, had offered me a lift to nearest restaurant. M Bouchard served a *pineau des Charentes* (mixture of seventy-five per cent local grape-juice and twenty-five per cent cognac; apparently a serendipitous discovery, like madeira, blotting paper, America, radio-activity etc). A drainage engineer, he'd worked on drilling-rigs in Africa, Oceania, South America (his favourite). He criticized the French colonial system for replacing all local institutions, compared to the British system of ruling indirectly, through whatever institutions were already in place. I admired two stuffed birds. He used to shoot, but couldn't stand the social life of the shooting club – banquets, drinking and boasting sessions, glad-handing everyone. On both these counts he must be unique among Frenchmen. He drove me to restaurant too, though I walked back in the dark. (Ten days later I flew back to the UK over this region. From five miles up the variegated countryside – dark green forests, bright yellow squares of colza, winding rivers – looks wonderful.) **25km**

Day 45: Breakfast. M Bouchard had gone out, which gave the others – Madame and a young lodger who was a designer at nearby factory – a chance. We talked of families rather than colonial systems. She had run the *chambre d'hôte* as something to do while he was away working. 'All our old friends are divorced,' she said sadly. 'They couldn't stand the separation.' Now he was retired, and at a loose end. A man of action, always in need of something to be doing. But there was room, and work, for an army here and in the outbuildings, and the guests bring variety to the conversation. He needed them now even more than she used to.

Into Angoulême, in weather swinging between interminable rain and endless sunshine. Well, it was April. More and more that was typical of the south-west. Here it was the growing frequency of rugby posts in the stadiums. Rugby is very much a regional game in France. There are whole swathes of northern and eastern France where you won't see a single pitch. The south-west, Ovalie, as it's sometimes called, is the heartland.

I remember Angoulême (from 1956) as hot (it was August), long, dusty, empty, sleepy, unmaintained. It was still long, but like all provincial French towns had otherwise changed utterly, with bypasses, parks, pedestrian precincts, and a prosperous bustle. The cathedral has striking sculptures – restored – on the west front, though you have to stand in the road to see them properly. Isabelle d'Angoulême was (our) King John's wife. Though engaged to the Count of Lusignan, she was carried off at the age of fourteen by John. When he died sixteen years later she went straight back to marry her former fiancé. There's a big statue to the assassinated President, Sadi Carnot (it's the spitting image of Cummings in *The Diary of a Nobody*). My mother-in-law, a *Sétoise,* once showed me the baker's shop in Sète where the anarchist Caserio lived. One day in 1894 he finished baking, took the train to Lyon, where the blameless President was opening an exhibition, jumped into his open carriage and stabbed him to death. Unsurprisingly, although he lived and worked in Angoulême, there was no statue here to Ravaillac, the mad would-be monk who, in 1610, assassinated the French king Henri IV. He went to Paris after work, jumped on the royal carriage and stabbed the king to death.

I found a comfortable brasserie run by two or three elderly gays (to judge solely by prissy gait and slightly overdone mannerisms). The waiter had no peripheral vision and was entirely without that precise, rapid silence of trained waiters. More *café* music – *Pretty Woman, Only yoooooo, Wherever you go,* and then at long last, Brassen's *Chanson pour l'Auvergnat (Elle est à toi, cette chanson*). The so-called *exception culturelle,* known here as *l'exception française*, allows the French to avoid American music by insisting that between 8am and 8pm seventy per cent of music on French radio must be by French artists. But they seem to take little notice of their exception. French popular music is quite unexportable, and they don't seem to listen to it themselves much, despite packing L'Olympia for Johnny Hallyday concerts.

A man at the bar used the phrase '*un musée de pédés*' (a queers' museum). Had I heard right? Yes, a minute later he said '*bande de pédés*'(bunch of queers). The man next to him murmured a protest. 'I said *bande de médés*' (doctors) claimed the first; they had indeed been talking about doctors. What a wag he must believe himself! I bet he has another bar for evenings, where he boasts of how he takes the piss at lunch-times. Most customers were regulars. A husband came in from work, sat opposite his wife, shook hands with the waiter, grabbed *en passant* the buttock of the woman at the next table, shook hands with her husband......Ah! ze Frrrrench! Excellent couscous.

There was a crisis in the Charente vineyards, I read. Only one third of the production was needed for cognac. The big cognac houses had laid down stocks for the next ten years. The French government spent £4 million last year on paying growers to root up their vines and change to other crops; one third of them had done so. Also typical of French government was that instead of merely leaving market forces to work, ie putting several thousand voters out of work, they were also trying to work through the structures in place (why didn't they do this in the colonies, as M Bouchard would have liked? No voters there perhaps). Producers' co-operatives, cognac makers and shippers, unions; all sides were brought together. There's always been a problem of overproduction of wine. Because vines live so long, and old ones produce best, it's impossible when they're planted to predict the eventual market. The paper was full of other such insights and useless information. House prices in town were less than a fifth of those in Brighton; fascinating (because I didn't understand them) details of cattle-prices – calves, various weights and breeds of heifer, cows that had, or had not, been 'taken to the bull'.

Angoulême is twinned with Hildesheim (Germany), Bury (Lancashire), Vitoria (Spain), Chicoutimi (Quebec, which many French believe to be a country) and other towns. It runs a well-known festival of strip-cartoons (an art form in France) every January. Anything in France may have its festival. Most are music-based, though often with a bias – jazz (Marciac, Vienne, Nice), techno (Montpellier), classical (Aix-en-Provence). Blues, rock, dance, folk, Latin-American, brass-band – all have their festivals. The visual arts are not far behind – photography, mime, street-arts, puppets, cinema. Some try to attract by their uniqueness. Dieppe has kite-flying, Lorient has the massive *Interceltique* for all Celts. And then there are the simply off-beat – festivals for heresies, bilberries, oysters, grass.

In the town-centre wives were keeping their husbands in order by taking them shopping, as opposed to simply buying what they wanted at prices they could afford. On the way out of town I saw my favourite graffiti of all time. Instead of the usual dogs-at-a-lamp-post effect achieved by taggers, this one said:

Là, tout n'est qu'ordre et beauté,
Luxe, calme et volupté.

There, all is order and beauty,
Luxury, tranquillity and voluptuousness

It's from Baudelaire's *L'Invitation au Voyage*. My epigraph!

From the bar I spotted four walkers, all women, with boots, cagoules. Later I passed them anxiously consulting map at village crossroads – roadworks had messed up all the waymarks. I strode confidently past with a cheery '*Bonjour!*' They didn't follow. Spring had ground to a halt, I waited forty-five minutes in freezing bus-shelter for the hotel to open. Cold smoulder of a sunset. The bar life was exotic, as always. Four men were telling drinking stories, the barman displayed his new cocktail, the black cook arrived for work, an old peasant entered with a bucket of eggs and was applauded, two men discussed how to mend a window-pane. I nearly got a heart-attack from an Alsatian, as I passed, in non-walking gear, within a foot of 'his' gate. I was so fed-up, I barked right back, quite shook the beast, yelled for anyone in the house to come and remove this threat to the highway. No answer of course. Neat little church – someone had heard of pointed arches, and tried to copy them in the tower window, but without real conviction – they're carved from a single block of stone.

Dinner – how just the opposite of everywhere else! We all sat at the same table, manager, cook, two friends, two workmen, me. Dishes and wine were shared round. *Hors d'oeuvres (*beetroot, tomatoes, carrot, vinaigrette), steak, pasta, salad, cheese-tray, dessert (a choice). Wine/water ad lib. £6, 8 euros. Wheeee! **18km**

Day 46: All the above were at work by the time I breakfasted. Tables were already laid for lunch, *c* forty people. 'Same every day,' said the manager. I asked why the hotel wasn't in the *topoguide*. 'Locals are simply lazy,' he claimed. 'And backbiting.' 'And boring.' So why did he stay, so far from his native Alsace? Vague answers of 'I'm OK here.' 'The countryside.' He mended a chair with furious, ill-directed, energy, complaining of wood, design, screws, screwdriver. 'It's the same everywhere,' I said in an attempt at solidarity. But he wouldn't have it. The chair was French, so no good; only in Germany were things done properly.

I sprayed my shoes with insect-repellent before setting off – at least it made them smell different. Despite some doomy prognostications in the *topoguide*, I'd no trouble with the path, at first anyway. Freezing wind and occasional rain were worse deterrents. Indeed I had to be reminded by cuckoos, oilseed rape, a shouting thrush etc, that it was April, not February. But the landscape was taking on some feature, much needed after the last few days. There were rock-shelters along steep wooded valleys. One hamlet consisted entirely of an old church, now a barn, another old ecclesiastical building, now another barn, several ruins, and a trim suburban villa with lawns and leylandii. *Palombière* in the woods – a tower for shooting wood pigeons from – with tame decoys in a cage at the foot. Pigeons are an agricultural pest everywhere. More than 1,000 grains of wheat have been counted in the crop of a single bird, and up to 130 acorns in another bird. But these *palombières* are to decoy migrating birds. Brussels banned the shooting of migrating birds as early as 1979, and there are far fewer *palombières* than there used to be, but the French government prefers to pay the fines rather than enforce the law. Other, less harmful and less numerous birds, such as turtle doves, continue to be massacred too. It's a tradition, you see.

I'd stopped looking at *lavoirs* (too few, none in use), horseshoes (no

Everywhere there were bonfires, men clearing and felling . . .

change), donkeys (none), woodpiles (far too many, it was enough to make you weep; everywhere the noise of chainsaws was heard in the land, everywhere there were bonfires, men clearing and felling). I was getting tired very quickly, stumbling in rutted lanes, and sitting down wherever it was dry. But everything was waterlogged – ruts, grass, hedges, fields, woodland, my shoes. At last I discovered an advantage of the wet; you could follow tracks. Footprints in the mud and, more than once today, bike trails in the grass. Why did I never see these phantom footpath-users?

Villebois-Lavalette showed up suddenly, surprising by its authority. A fort, a château, a church on a steep conk, with the village spilling down to the plain. In the evening sun I walked up the street past a huge old covered market with stone stalls, to the château. It was closed, nothing was visible through gaps in the planks of the gate. There was no memorial to Count Georges-Henri de Villebois-Mareuil, colonel in the Foreign Legion, and organiser of the French volunteers who fought with the Boers. He became a general, before being killed at the battle of Boskop, near Potchefstroom. Back in the UK, within reach of an encyclopaedia, I discovered that, despite his name, he'd no connection with this part of the country. Titles!

'Weather will get better tomorrow,' old gossip in street *dixit*. Tiny wizened rowdy peasants homeward plodded their weary way at nine thirty. And so did I. **25km**

Day 47: Overcast, odd drops. Waymarks fickle. *Topoguide* disappointing, it sometimes read as if it had been compiled from the map, not on the ground. And it was certainly out-of-date. Maps, waymarks and common sense were best. One sign read *CHEMIM (sic) DE RANDONNEE* but it was the right path. The *café* in La Rochebeaucourt-et-Argentine (name and a half!) was full of a Thomas Hardy type chorus – four old peasants in dog-track cloth-caps or Lenin/sailor caps, and three younger men who chipped in to keep the pot boiling. I snuggled up to a hot stove.

Several frontiers were crossed today, the most important being the least tangible, that between the Langue d'oïl and the Langue d'oc. In the Middle Ages, north and west of this line the word for 'yes' was *'oïl'*, whence *'oui'*; south and east of here, the word was *'oc'*. This was only the most obvious difference of many, and despite the victory of the north in imposing its language as the national one, the difference still shows through in pronunciation and vocabulary. From now on, I'd find that the final 'e' of words like *vite, Toulouse, femme* etc was pronounced. In daily vocabulary *'fada'* is 'crazy', *escamper*, to throw something away, *rouméguer*, to grumble and many, many more.This was the France I know best and am most at home in. Relax and smile, it's the sunny south!

Somewhere between Villebois and Mareuil, too, ran the *ligne de démarcation.* In 1940, the Germans took all the north, and the Atlantic seaboard, under their direct rule, leaving Vichy-governed 'France' with about one third of its territory. 'A bit in the mouth of France' said a German at the time, and they only had to twitch the reins to remind who was in control. Passes were needed for every crossing; goods needed endless papers. Divide and rule.

I also crossed from Charente into Dordogne. And finally, there was a geological change. To reach Argentine, the second half of the village, I had to climb on to a *causse*, a weathered limestone plateau, a karst, the first of many. The *causses* are lovely walking country - rabbit-nibbled turf, with brilliant spring flowers, distant views, well-drained. I strode happily along on what was marked on the map as 'aerodrome'. In fact the GR was the runway. Then towards scrubby oakwoods, along traces of the Roman road from Spain to Brittany. It ran this far east, away from the marshy coast and wide river-crossings, as the Romans needed massive, swift, reliable transfer of infantry. There were paving-stones with the tell-tale ruts of more recent cartwheels. And then I arrived at a long-disused railway; ghosts of travellers of 2000 years buzzed around my ears.

Up on to a treeless plateau in glacial rain and wind. Suddenly there was a bus-shelter, with a seat. Ah! Twenty minutes later the rain had stopped, and it was sunny. In the windless woodland, I was hot. I followed roe-deer tracks past châteaux, two village churches, then took the tarmac to Mareuil. The *lavoir* in fine condition, though not used; there was an A4 analysis of the non-drinkable water posted on the wall, though. In Mareuil was a memorial to five 'victims of German barbarity', of 1944. No political correctness here, and quite right. Later reactions may be different, but we should not falsify the original ones.

More *causse* in the afternoon, interrupted twice by patches of gale-felled woodland. These were conifers, which were even trickier to negotiate than deciduous. The second lot in particular cost a lot of time, perhaps thirty minutes for each 100 metres. Clouds reappeared, and I reached the hotel only just in time to avoid a storm – wind, downpour, lightning, the whole works. Wouldn't everything be wet tomorrow! From my room the lake, the black dripping trees, the deserted chairs and tables, gave a fine impression of a small, not very fashionable German spa, out of season. The trees were covered in mosses and lichens, presumably the air was so clean. Suddenly a last, horizontal, ray of sunshine on birches, and it was young green spring.

In the restaurant, there were family groups, commercial groups, three Brits, from whom I felt further removed than from any. They discussed who wanted to rent which château, what a pity so-and-so who lived in the stables couldn't afford to maintain the chapel, which craftsmen could be trusted with the restoration of cherished wardrobes, and so on. Well, it takes all sorts, I thought easily, but then…. 'The first time, I was unfaithful while we were engaged,' said one suddenly, 'but with the second husband, never.' And 'the', not 'my'!? You don't do that where I come from, and if you do, you certainly don't talk about it. Two other Brits, monoglots, left. *'Buenas noches, amigos,'* said one, showing off his foreign. If I didn't have a varied and enjoyable inner life, I'd not survive this solitude. It makes some people desperate for any company, but in me it breeds paranoia and misanthropy. To counter this, I need constant listening, as well as phoning home every two days. But I was still surprising myself by my aptitude for solitude. Probably my family and friends recognise this already, though I was dismayed. There were three dogs and a cat in the restaurant. It wasn't that they begged, barked, jumped on your table or grabbed your dinner. No, they just walked up and down smelling each other's bums. Some people must have found this more acceptable. **27km**

Day 48: Clear, chilly, autumnal still. The restaurateur was one of those men who think to increase the joviality content of the universe by laughing all the time. He offered me a lift down to the village, told me of an eighty-year old walker (English; they all are) who had booked the next night's hotel in Gramat, 130km away. Weren't these stories getting out-of-hand?

Brantôme, dominated by an eleventh century abbey

I walked down to the village, on the way notching up 1000km, then short-cut up long valley to Léguillac-de-Cercles, arriving in a sharp shower. Hamlet of La Verrerie had solid well-designed farmhouses, with neatly-carved ornaments. This is pre-history country, with rock shelters in every little valley, private, green, isolated. I got to one shelter just in time to avoid the worst of a downpour. Me and Neanderthal Man! But it was April, and within five minutes, I was down to shirtsleeves again, in leafless woodland. Pond – well, a glorified roadside ditch really – of which one end was a solid pack of tadpoles. Near the middle were one or two with four legs already, strangely elongated. And two adults clutching an underwater branch. Poked them with my stick. They were newts, 12-15cm long. Great Crested? I removed ivy from the waymarked trees, on the same principle as mountain-walkers add stones to cairns.

Into Brantôme. Ragged cumulus raced across the sky. Bells sounded from the abbey dominating the island town.

Towery city, and branchy between towers,
Bell-swarmed . . . rook-racked, river-rounded

Wild iris was flowering on a bank by the abbey, too steep for pickers. Firemen were practising abseiling from a third-storey window of the abbey. I passed, twice, a real tramp, with huge greasy back-pack, dogs and dreadlocks, once begging, once visiting supermarket. Never a kind word for his dogs. I felt uncomfortably fake, but thanked goodness I was not dressed as a walker, either time. Laboratory studies have shown that subjects are greatly cheered when they meet others much worse off in some way; glad to find that my heart didn't rise too much. The fact that I was merely 'playing' at being a vagabond was both a comfort and an embarrassment.

This was definitely the Languedoc. I saw three memorials round town to local *félibres*, poets and writers in Occitan. The greatest was Frédéric Mistral, from Provence though, not Périgord; Nobel prize winner in 1904 and still, I believe, the only one not to have written in a national language. He'd been proposed for the prize the year before, but the French government was horrified at the idea of honouring a

French writer who wrote not in French but in Provençal, 'a patois good only for shepherds'. What! Provençal the language of the troubadours fit only for shepherds? They put enough pressure on the Swedish Academy to have him rejected in favour of Bjornsterne Bjornson. No doubt Mistral was cheered by the thought that Ibsen, Tolstoy and Strindberg were also passed over. However, the Swedes returned to the charge in 1904, and French pressure this time could only ensure that Mistral did not win outright, but shared with the Spaniard David Etchegaray, mathemetician and dramatist – best-known, like too many Nobel prize-winners for literature, for being unheard-of. It was also Mistral who invented the name Mireille, and persuaded a registrar to give it official status.

Ten donkeys were for sale in the paper; what a snip at £3,000! Another in a field today was calming two thoroughbreds simply by doing so very much less than they were. I had a beer in the sunshine, wrote postcards, rested my legs. Wives were keeping their husbands in order by emerging from the florist's and asking what they thought of their hair-dos. Had they had one? In the florist's? When? Panic set in. At about this time Huguette whizzed past, perhaps ten kilometres above me, on her way to Toulouse where I was to meet her on Monday.

The French children in the restaurant were no trouble at dinner-time, except to their parents with constant questions: 'Will there be chips?', 'Why can't I start with ice-cream?' The parents went on talking, eating, smoking, round/over/between them. Grandparents fed the smaller ones. The children remained seated, their interjections into the conversation were answered; nobody felt a need to apologise for them. There *was* no need to apologise for them. In the back room of the restaurant, something was going on though. More than fifty people went through , singly or in groups. Later that night, 1.15pm in fact, there were shouts in the street as they were ushered out and dispersed. Two or three were back at 3.30pm, loudly trying to remember where they had parked. **25km**

Day 49 promised to be the longest yet, though I'd spotted a 6km short-cut. Breakfast in the bar, with decorated mirrors advertising bygone *apéritifs*. The noise last night turned out to have been the annual cards competition, *belote* of course. The third prize was a sheep. 'Alive?' I asked. Madame looked at me as though I was a simpleton, which perhaps I was being. 'Dead,' she said precisely. 'Cut up.' *Belote*, whose rules are far too complicated to give here, is, like markets and village fetes, an essential ingredient of *la France profonde*. Others include the *Opinel* or *Laguiole*, a rough-handled, single-bladed knife with which you eat holding food in other hand and cutting off chunks against the thumb (and wearing a beret). Cheese, *saucisson*, fruit, onions, bread, all go this way. I've even heard of a wedding reception at which the men in the bride's family took them out in preference to the laid-on best silverware. It's for males only, like pissing by the roadside. You can prefer not to participate in this, but another ingredient of *la France profonde, le loto* (bingo), is open to all. Re-usable cards, with little markers such as grains of maize, or dried beans. It's a social rather than a financial occasion, so rather slow, and often played for a line of five numbers (*quine*), not all fifteen numbers (*carton complet*). Like us, callers give the numbers nicknames, such as department numbers: 34 is Hérault, 88 Vosges, etc. Then 51 is Pastis, 80 Chasseurs (it's a song), 33 Docteur (why?). One is *un, tout seul*; not *l'oeil de Quély*, I'm sorry to say. You can announce success in any way you like, by shouting *J'ai!* or *Quine!* or *Carton!* or *Oui!* or by just screaming. In one game there was huge excitement when a prize of duck *avec foie gras* was misheard by many as *avec Viagra*. If you're too old to hear the difference, you need it.

For the third, and not the last time, when the bill came, I had to remind about a drink taken in the bar the evening before, and overlooked. What's happening to the money-conscious French? Down a river for once, though for only a few kilometres. Then a treeless plain, with heavier and heavier rain. Amazingly there was a bus-shelter again. No stop, no sign, just the shelter. I saw only three of these shelters, and two of them saved me from a real soaking. I'd forgotten to fill my water bottle again, and the only shop I passed was shut (it was Sunday). Plenty of rain, though, provided an endless supply of clean puddle-water. Perhaps I should have carried a straw. I lost my way several times – waymarkers: *nul point!* Serious difficulties in the gale-wrecked forest, the worst damage I'd seen.

Elsewhere,

The woods are lovely, dark and deep,
But I have promises to keep
And miles to go before I sleep

Le Figaro was running a headline this weekend, *Hors des Sentiers Battus (*Off the Beaten Track), about the joys of rambling. Naturally I didn't meet a single rambler. I sheltered from the rain in the hotel bar in Chancelade, along with an off-duty waiter and two motorcyclists who'd spent a wet weekend at the Le Mans 24-hour motorcycle rally. Why don't the French Ramblers organize a 24-hour ramble round that site of pilgrimage?

Everyone who came in smelled of wet dog, except the sensible dog, which smelled of dry dog. The barman told us how scared he had been during the gale, and said that many elderly people were depressed and frightened by any strong wind since then. Eventually we all wished each other '*Bon courage!*' and dashed severally off into the rain. Legs terrific, I just bounced along. And the rain abated. I splashed through the roadside puddles into Périgueux, saved from a severe soaking by it being Sunday, when French HGVs are not allowed to travel. Today's wildlife was a giant whiskery square-headed rat by a suburban pond. Coypu? Muskrat?

Relaxed with my feet in the hotel bidet. The bidet is the perfect example of an invention misunderstood by its inventors. The French believe it's for washing bums, though they often have a shower alongside, I notice. This idea has even gained some currency among francophile Brits. But its real use is as a footbath. You can do nothing with your feet in a shower, starting with reaching them. They just stand there, silent, in the dirty water, like two donkeys in the rain. But pull up a chair by the bidet, and smother your feet in hot soapy water, stroking and kneading. Ahhhhhh...... The restaurant served enterprising vegetables – pumpkin soup, Jerusalem artichokes, parsnips; these are rarities in France. Everyone knows the French eat snails, frogs' legs, horsemeat, but it's less well-known that they hardly ever eat many things we find delicious, like elderberries, baked potato-skins, swedes, pork crackling, ginger, gooseberries, baked beans, piccalilli, as well as those above. Room for some missionary endeavour here? **33km**

Next day I took the train to Toulouse, chuntering along at three to four foot-days per hour.

5

June – Périgueux to Castelnaudary

My sister Chris and her husband George Hart had found time to come and join me for a few days – this had been part of the original plan, last year. We had booked into a little hotel in Sarliac.

Day 50: We took the school bus into Périgueux. There were no children, as everyone was making the Friday a *pont* between the Thursday of Ascension and the weekend. The bus took us to Périgueux bus station, but I was not leaving any gaps, however small, so we asked the driver for directions to the SNCF station. Generously, he drove us there. It was a beautiful sunny morning, unlike the torrential rain of my April visit. George navigated us with his customary decisiveness out through the suburbs to the GR 36 on the hills north of the town. In Champcevinel we resisted a visit to the bar on the reasonable grounds that it was only 10.30am. There was a plaque by the war memorial to two RAF Mosquito aircrew downed here in August 1944. Just as in Moncé-en-Belin (Day 28) a street had been called after them. The roads gradually turned into lanes, then tracks, then our way lay through woods and along field edges. When we were only half a mile from our next landmark, the mediaeval fortress of Caussade, the path led us into an ambush. The hillside was strewn with pines felled by the December gales, sometimes up to six lying across one another. There must have been several hundred in all, and it took well over an hour to clamber through/between/up/under/round/over/along/down/off them. I fell 3m backwards off one, and scraped both legs. Found a patch of shade just in time to sit down before shock attacked, leaving me shaky and uncertain. It was now 30°C in the shade, and the hillside was in full sunshine. Finally, at the top, we collapsed under some still-standing trees. I said 'Not bad for a combined age of 186.' We laughed hysterically for a minute.

At the fortress, a very fine relic of the Hundred Years War, a cuckoo was calling in exact timing with its echo from the walls – cuckoo*cuckoo*, cuckoo*cuckoo*. We crossed more woodland, regaining strength and morale, but now suffering from heat and lack of a bar. The main road was full of lorries so we detoured via Château les Bories, with a full moat, complete with waterfowl and windows that looked as though they'd been missing since the Revolution. Then we gritted our teeth and plodded along the main road to the first bar, where we recuperated for an hour. After that, the last few kilometres, along the road back to our hotel, were bearable, especially as we were recognised and hooted at by one of the waitresses passing in her car. 'You were walking really fast!' she said later. The image of walkers in France is strange – they're regarded as eccentrics, probably marginal to society, but simultaneously as athletes. Behind the bar was a sketch of a tramp, with sack and stick, captioned, 'He gave his customers credit.'

We dined outside in the twilight, under a nest-box, which a curious finger proved to be empty. Not for long, though, as a giant hornet droned past on its way in to build. Chris has heard an explanation about horseshoes, from Brittany. If they're hung U, it allows the devil to sit in them, so hang them inverted. **18km**

Day 51: A short sharp shower at the exact moment we set foot outside the door. Chris drove with baggage to lunchtime rendezvous; George and I walked along soft, warm, shady paths. A well-intentioned driver attempted to show us the wrong way. Chestnut woods, meadow-sweet. Wooded path above the Auvézère brought us to Le Change. A group of people was gathering in the village, some of their cars with out-of-department numbers (wedding, christening?); we circled the church, sat down at a bar. A priest arrived in full fig. The barman explained it was the funeral of the baker's grandmother, who used to live here. Black is out for funerals these days, not one of the hundred or so people was wearing it, though all were in sombre greys or browns, and all were hatless. Bells (they're hung the other way up from in England) tolled, the hearse pulled in, pall-bearers loaded up, visitors signed the book of condolences by the church door. Most people followed the coffin inside, but several made straight for the bar.

At the next village, Blis-et-Born, the fête was in preparation (*pétanque* competition, snail dinner, torchlight procession, then dancing tomorrow). This is the country of Bertrans de Born, mediaeval troubadour and stirrer-up of strife, notably between Henry II and his sons Richard the Lionheart and John Lackland. But a great poet in an age when military skill, troublemaking, and writing great love poetry could acceptably co-exist in one personality.

We met Chris at the appointed spot, lunched, then she took over from George. We set a rendezvous in the next village, but despite signs to '*Chez Momo*' there was no bar (and anyway if that stood for Mohamed it wasn't going to serve beer). In now sweltering pre-storm closeness we passed an extraordinary new house as shown in *Megalomaniacs Monthly*, big in every possible way, showy, over-decorated, standing in the middle of a bare hillside where it implored the passing tribute of a gawp. At the hotel George had unloaded bags and had a round of drinks waiting – shandies to start with, then beer; this turned out to be a good pattern. A couple of kilometres to the east are the truffle nurseries of Ajat, where spores of the famous black truffle of Perigord are fixed by a secret process to the roots of an appropriate sapling, which is then planted. After that you wait. Fellow-guests were two parties of Dutch. One was of four young men in a minibus, with drum-kits; the other, a middle-aged couple, had just flooded the staircase by blocking the shower outlet. There was an unnerving story in the paper, on the Aquitaine pages too, about five dogs which had broken out of their garden and killed an old lady walking past. Their owners were being prosecuted for manslaughter. **20km**

The waymarked van

Day 52: George had to get up in the night to silence the Dutch drummers who were cavorting on the balcony at 2am. Nevertheless, after breakfast, he set a terrific pace. He's a whipcord ectomorph, while I'm an average sort of mesomorph, and his old training as leader of Ramblers' Society groups was still in evidence. Shouting 'Hiya, girls!' at groups of heifers, we covered 7km in just over an hour, short-cut to the GR, then across easy country. An abandoned Citroen van jammed into a thicket had red-and-white waymarks on it: nice one, waymarkers! So we rendezvoused early with Chris, then tackled the second section. And got lost. The path had changed, waymarks didn't exist. Finally, we found a road-sign and a telegraph pole with place-name attached (as French ones do); we were far to the north of where we should have been, so we tore along white roads to Fanlac church, arriving only just in time to stop Chris worrying. It turned out to have been only partly our mistake. We had taken the older of the two

Despite this waymark we were lost soon after

topoguides, without comparing the maps, which differ. The fact that the descriptive texts in the *topoguides* were identical merely compounded the confusion.

Fanlac was very home-counties rural, Swiss holiday homes, that sort of thing. Sandwich and beer at the restaurant put us in a much better frame of mind. Chris and I set out on the 6km remaining, down a nice steep rocky path to the valley floor, then up a nasty steep rocky path on the other side. A young man on a motorbike wanted to come past, but we outfaced him effortlessly. Again, the map and the guide disagreed at one point, but this time we were alert and it was no problem. Along grassy terrace path to Montignac, where our meeting place 'on the church steps' was confused by there being two churches. We waited by the first one till George arrived, having found a hotel. Going through town, I passed, without entering, an open secondhand bookshop. Self-denial or what? The hotel room had swish armchairs, but no hot water till 6pm; this must be tourist country. Perhaps in reaction to my explanations of obscure points of French syntax, George regaled us with stories of the Patent Office in the 1950s. 'You have total recall of everything before our marriage,' said Chris, a tad tartly. I sent off a flock of postcards – nano-splinters of immortality. **28km**

Day 53: The cave-paintings at nearby Lascaux are now permanently closed to the public, to prevent the environmental damage caused by warmth and breath and, guess what, the two rooms of replicas, which tourists can see, are closed on Mondays. Still, we'd already seen those of Niaux, in the Pyrenees, where the originals, almost as good as those of Lascaux, are still on view to the public, though probably not for long. Hurry! Both Chris and George, on their non-walking stints yesterday, had noticed a plaque at a château near Fanlac, recording the imprisonment of French communists, trade-unionists etc from

Memorial plaque for the Camp du Sablou

January to December 1940, when they were deported to North Africa; a curious continuity of policy between the Third Republic and its successor, the collaborating Vichy government. I discovered later that there were several of these camps. Those 'deported' were the supposed troublemakers, as conditions in the Algerian camps were harder. But imprisonment by the Germans would have been much, much, worse; many lives were saved by the move.

George and I worked our way through woodland, much hampered by some appallingly sticky mud, past a pre-historic zoo (a zoo with the sort of animals that might have been found here in 10,000BC – primitive sheep, bison, Przewalski's horse etc. No woolly rhinoceros, mammoths, or sabre-toothed tigers. Good!) A baby vole, very non-prehistoric, scuttled across the path. As we sat down with Chris and a well-earned beer at St Léon-sur-Vézère, two people crossed the road towards us with wide 'Hello!'s. A coincidence. They were from Maisons-Laffitte near Paris, as are the Harts, whom they knew from the Anglican church there.

Then four Americans, who had been inspecting the restaurant menu and heard us speaking English, wanted to know how to order *omelette aux cèpes* (wild mushrooms) without the *cèpes*. This is like black velvet without the champagne, or bacon-and-eggs without the bacon, or the eggs. Manfully, we told them though. We sat for another half-hour to see who might turn up next.

In the next patch of woodland some joker had put up a sign saying HOTEL about 5km from anywhere, and graffiti-ed a wall *Lama=Tibet=Secte.* Eh? Later in Le Moustier, though, there was a sign to DHAGPO KAGYU LING. I discovered later that there is indeed a lamasery – the centre of French Buddhism. Although there had been some bad feeling between the locals and the incomers in the 1980s – whence the graffiti - it had died down, especially since the visit of the Dalai Lama in 1991. Currently there are several monks, and some hundreds of summer visitors. We also passed a notice discouraging us from touching any fawns we might come across – the mother abandons them.

We visited the huge, 900m long rock-terrace of St Christophe. Halfway up a 200m cliff overlooking the river, this has an extraordinary history. Neanderthal remains from 70,000BC have been found here, and almost every succeeding culture occupied this natural fortress. A Neolithic skull from 8000BC can be seen, with Bronze and Iron Age relics. The terrace was fortified against Viking raiders in 976 by the bishop of Périgueux. There was a horn-blown alarm system running from cliff-shelter to cliff-shelter up the river to give adequate notice to dash home with children and livestock, pull up the ladders, and guard the entry. It was inhabited, by up to 3000 people, in the Hundred Years War and the French Wars of Religion (1560-1598), before being made uninhabitable at the order of the king. You can see the remains of a church, hoists, a communal kitchen, guard-rooms, water-tanks, animal sheds, a slaughterhouse. Ladders and bridges could be pulled up or burnt. Many similarities with the Indian towns of Mesa Verde in Colorado.

On the way back to the hotel we picked up two bags of baby green walnuts for pickling. We were offered soup yet again; often it's the spicy tomato *tourin* of Périgord, but sometimes undifferentiated vegetable. And, unlike Paris, at the end of the meal, we were always asked, '*Vous avez terminé?*' never the fashionable '*Ça a été?*' **22km**

Day 54: Chris had sore toes through wearing wrong shoes on the first day, and volunteered for the driving. George and I took the path down (at last!) the river, which meanders gracefully, each loop guarded by a castle or village. As we whizzed through oakwoods on a narrow path, we met a couple watching birds, who turned out to be British walkers but not birdwatchers at all, on tour with Headwater, an organisation that ferries your bags to the next hotel while you walk, with just the day's needs. Dropping down to the SNCF station in Les Eyzies to meet Chris for lunch, we came upon a small rock-shelter. Suddenly I saw a discreet plaque. This was the rock-shelter of Cro-Magnon, which has given its name to the type of man (among the earliest examples of Homo sapiens, long-headed, tall, big-brained), who succeeded Neanderthal Man in these parts and whose remains were discovered here in 1868. There were skeletons of three men, one woman, and a foetus, from 30,000 to 40,000 years ago. What were they doing here? How did they die?A posh hotel and its outbuildings hid the shelter from view, and it was not sign-posted. The bones are in a museum, and here where our earliest recognisable ancestors lived and died, all there is to see is through the imagination. George got excited by the rural trains, and rushed off to take photos, while Chris and I sank beers, the expense of which was partly attenuated by excellent green olives.

Up a fine path out of Les Eyzies, and we were lost immediately; blundering about for a full half-hour before finding the track. Quite different from, and much less pleasant than, this morning's paths. Numbers of Dutch and British houses among the trees. A surveyor was measuring a giant wood-pile, with a view to deciding who owned how much. Suddenly we realised our watch had stopped, and sprinted down an almost vertical slope into St Cyprien, where a lone figure reading on the church steps turned into Chris. The church has some connection with Bertrand de Got, Pope Clement V. The street leading up is called after him too. He was the Pope who moved the Papacy from Rome to Avignon in 1309, helped the French king suppress the Templars, and excommunicated Robert the Bruce. But he was neither born nor died here, nor was he the bishop. Cyprien himself was a local sixth century monk and hermit and not, as I had thought, a Tunisian bishop. Well, there you go. The day's wildlife was a tiny shrew, dead on the path. In the hotel our fellow-guests were a coach-load of OAPs on an outing. They even had a sing-song organised for them that evening. **21km**

Plaque at the Cro-Magnon rock shelter

Day 55: Along the Dordogne, past three parked army buses, on what would be the towpath if such a thing were here possible. It never has been, because of the hugely variable water-level. Today a heavy swirling current was snatching at the lower branches of many of the trees. The mere sound of purling water, as George said, reduces the heat by ten degrees. A woman was spraying potatoes – yes, she said, it was for Colorado beetle, a word that struck terror in Britain when I was young. If you ever came across one you were supposed to accompany it to the nearest police station to assist the police in their enquiries. On this rich alluvial soil, *jardins potagers* (kitchen gardens) were flourishing. So neat, so full! Lines of chubby cabbages, leeks, onions, alternate with glossy chard or sorrel, with frondy carrots and asparagus, with dark-veined beetroot, purple aubergines, plump pumpkins, with lettuce, round or upright, oak-leaved or red (my favourite is called *Grosse Blonde Paresseuse*, Big Lazy Blonde), peas and tomatoes on their supports. All in close rows, with barely room to pass between. There are clumps of parsley, chives, mint, courgettes, rhubarb. Serious fencing, often with tin-cans to protect the tops of the wooden posts.

At Allas-les-Mines, across the bridge came a column of soldiers, of all ages and conditions, on a route-march. Children and grandmothers waved, village dogs strode proudly out alongside. Another column 200m behind. All wished us '*Bonjour!*' They were on the left of the road, I was glad to see, facing the oncoming traffic. The French have taken a long time to realise that their universal law of keeping to the right is so dangerous for pedestrians. Off went the soldiers towards their buses. We sat in a small public garden to make our farewells, as the Harts were returning to Paris to fulfil previous engagements. Their house is a hotbed of hospitality. Chris, who'd been scampering gamely alongside the much longer-legged George and me, was complaining of bruised toes still.

With a full rucksack for once, I started alone up the hill where, as was becoming a habit, I lost the GR. But it was no problem – there were little roads everywhere, all empty. Cows came over to watch me. Cars go too fast to bother with, but walkers are recognisable and as mysterious to them as comets.

While I was lunching on the square in St Germain-de-Belvès (a rather grand way of saying I sat in the shade of the *mairie* notice-board nibbling a bun), three American women questioned me keenly about my walk, while being curiously evasive about themselves. Despite discreet questions, I didn't learn where they were staying, why their car was registered in Nice, what they were doing here, where they came from even. Local phone boxes were of wood, with steep tiled square roofs, to match the local architecture. One even had a directory! Drystone walls, stone 'beehives' (circular storage sheds in fields) and dovecotes were everywhere; and splendidly compact hamlets (Lolivarie was one) with the houses all touching, and many-angled roofs. A man pruning roses wished me '*Bon voyage!*'. Later he overtook me on the lane and offered me a lift to Belvès. No thank you, of course. Anglo influence – bar advertising darts, and a horseshoe U. But this may be something more interesting. Last year, at a demonstration of iron-forging near Foix, I was delighted to hear the blacksmith claim that since good luck comes from heaven, horseshoes should be hung U in order to catch it. They were only inverted as it used a nail less. 'So go home and change them,' he addressed the crowd. Which of these two myths will prevail? Certainly neither is well-known, though iron to protect against fairies is a very old tradition. Horseshoes on the door were to prevent them from entering, and stealing or 'changing' babies.

That evening in the hotel restaurant there were screams from the kitchen, where the prettier of the waitresses was getting her bottom pinched by the cook. Next time she emerged the British woman, two tables from mine, said: 'We wondered whether we should come and help you.' The girl looked blank, so the Brit gave a very fine scream herself, in explanation. The waitress blushed and fled, but could be heard laughing in the kitchen and re-imitating the scream. A very proper use of drama! **16km**

Day 56: A green-and-blue day, hot but humid. Slugs, puddles, dew, midges like cyclists' heels in the dark. France has, or used to have, the most centralised administration in Western Europe, and recent decentralisation has not led to fewer or simpler regulations. I saw from the morning's paper that log-transporters, with more work this year than ever before, have their maximum permitted axle-weights fixed by the *préfecture* of each department. So some could remove more of the gale-felled trees than others. Naturally there was a strike threatened.

In the morning, there were ten kilometres or so of well-signed forest track, rather open woodland in many parts, with ponds here and there.

Transhumance as it was

Transport as it was

Later, the GR turned into a nudist camp. The only three people I saw were fully clad but, in a rush of goodwill, I stifled the cries of 'Get your kit off, then' that rose to my lips, and withdrew half a mile to the main road. There was a liquid, shimmering luminosity, with an agreeable breeze, not yet the desiccating oven-breath of August. But it was at least 27°C, so I kept resting on the grass in the shade.

I arrived at a hotel/bar kept by four people at lunch. They greeted me in English (because of my T-shirt – 'Tour de France in Brighton'). French woman, Australian man, a young couple I'd guess to be bilingual. All too soon they rushed off to serve guests. Judicious short-cuts – the GR rambled hopelessly about – brought me hot and sweaty, bright pink and out of water, to Monpazier where, to my surprise, I was hailed by two cyclists. It was the two men from the lunchtime hotel, ostensibly out looking for mushrooms, but also, I'd guess, wondering whether my story was true. We enthused about small French roads for walking and cycling, wondered why so many Brits are mycophobes, then traffic hooted and they left. I wish I'd learnt more about them.

Monpazier is a *bastide* town, founded by the English in 1284. Both English and French wanted to settle an increasing, fluid, potentially unstable population, by building these fortified market towns. Almost 300 were envisaged, and many survive. Built on a gridiron plan round an arcaded central square with a covered market (that of Monpazier, in fourteenth century chestnut, still stands), narrow streets, a church, a fairground etc. All mod cons to tempt people to stay. Dinner out on the square, in the evening shadow. **26km**

Day 57: Over breakfast husbands were keeping their wives in order by reading them the newspaper headlines, summarising the articles, and providing closely-reasoned refutations. 'Yes, dear.'

Lanes and tracks at first –

Where you lean against a bank while a van passes
And the deep lane insists on the direction
Into the village . . .

I was running out of things to think about, despite Château de Biron, an impressive pile and Lacapelle-Biron, with nice friendly bar and department Resistance memorial. The next bit of GR had been waymarked by a clown; he marked at junctions, so that you knew you were on the right path but not which way to go. He lost me later in a wood, but by mid-afternoon I'd regained the GR, a shady terrace walk about ten feet above the flood-plain of a small river. The weather was getting closer and cloudier, sweltering. To pre-booked *chambre d'hôte* in Sauveterre-la-Lémance, run single-handed by M Salle, a widower. As I went to phone for next two nights' accommodation, I was alarmed to see a poster advertising *'Fêtes médiévales'* at my proposed next stop. And both hotels there were *complet.* Realised with a sudden jolt at my stupidity that it was Whit weekend – just like at Etretat last year. All reachable hotels/*chambres d'hôte/gîtes* were booked. Except the *gîte* at Cazès, which turned out to have closed three years ago. Composed angry letter to guide – this was the second piece of dud info that the *gîte* guide had given. But how could I have been so stupid? A sort of insane macho optimism, almost entirely without foundation in experience (though at the last two hotels, I had been virtually the sole guest).

M Salle suggested some possibilities, lent me his phone. He'd cooked *pâté*, *paella*, strawberry fool. He had worked as a *maître d'* in Paris for thirty-seven years, and in Bolton for one. He and his wife and six kids had restored a watermill near Moissac over many years, but sold it when he retired as being too isolated. They bought this house, which had belonged to the manager of the village factory when it had 200 employees. Now there are barely that number of inhabitants. His children were everywhere – St Petersburg, Dresden, one just across the road. He was very active, gardening, cooking, travelling, running the house. The week before he'd put up a party of twenty Swiss cyclists. We discussed small-town life in the Midi, and country life in general. He was sure the moon influences growth and quoted as examples lettuces, radishes, when you get your hair cut (it grows faster when the moon's waxing, he claimed). He got me to admit that if the moon could influence the tides, it might also influence living things consisting mainly of water, though he couldn't explain how. Many French gardeners believe you should plant vegetables that rise (lettuce, beans etc) when the moon is waxing, and those that descend (potatoes, turnips) when the moon is waning. I think secretly they believe that the moon is somehow bigger when it is full, and therefore exerts a greater pull. After all, someone did write to an English newspaper, asking why the Americans didn't fire their moon-shots when the moon was full, as it would offer a bigger target. We discussed census methods in UK and France, then talked about Quebec – he'd been, and found the locals very welcoming, but not easy to understand because of their accent, and still more, their vocabulary. He was worried about the whole world speaking English. I consoled him by pointing out that the wider a language spreads, the harder it is for the speakers to understand each other – languages aren't infinitely elastic, as his experience in Quebec showed. Storm loomed larger, and broke as I went to bed. **25.5km**

Day 58: Decided on Plan B as I lay wide-awake at 4am. Over breakfast M Salle told me he'd been out collecting snails after the rain, how expensive lightning-conductors were, which trees had come down in the gales. We complained wittily about French administration. Less centralised than formerly, perhaps less so now than the English system, it is still slow, rigid, cumbersome – constipated is the classic adjective. A civil servant, and there are seven million of them, when asking for a day off, can't just clear things with his line-manager. He has to write a letter to the *préfet*, correctly formulated: *'Je sollicite de votre haute bienveillance.....'* ('I crave your indulgence in asking....'). Real eighteenth century stuff. He won't get an answer, either. Like many people in the hospitality business, M Salle avoided contradicting, or even presenting points of view that might offend, so he was rather too willing to agree to make a really first-class conversationalist. But he'd had a very varied experience, and had a great spread of knowledge. *'Chacun y trouve son compte'* he said of the *chambre d'hôte* system, as I made ready to go. Indeed it does suit both parties. I was fed, lodged, for £24; he had company and a subject for future conversations. There is a railway through the village, but the station closed two years ago, and no buses have replaced the trains. So he offered me a lift to Fumel. No. But when plan B, involving a 40km day, didn't work, as yet another hotel was full, I was forced to fall back on Plan C: walk to Fumel, bus to Cahors, come back and fill the gap later.

The rain had the decency to hold off for half an hour before closing in, and was then only a drizzle. I startled the barmaid at Bonaguil by arriving on foot: 'I didn't hear your car…' she exclaimed indignantly. But that's walking; you arrive suddenly, unannounced unless by dogs, surprising locals quietly gardening or meditating, by wishing them *Bonjour* out of the blue. The Château de Bonaguil is a last gasp of the expiring Middle Ages, but looked formidable as I went down the valley; certainly enough to scare off the few attackers who came up here before cannon were perfected and fortified châteaux went out of fashion. A one-eyed dog followed me for want of something better to do. He got the message after a bit, just like the hounds in Normandy had done. At Fumel everything was closed or closing. Locals tried to be helpful, but didn't really know much about the bus service. I missed the 12.30pm by about 50m as there was no bus stop sign. 'Yes, there used to be one, but they took it away,' said a helpful passer-by. The 14.00 didn't come at all. Dried off in bar as rain was now a glum, steady, downpour. Heard '*pastaga*', slang for a *pastis*, for the first time on the walk. Put my pullover on under the cagoule, but was still freezing.

Suddenly things started to go right. The clothes shop in whose doorway I'd been sheltering and changing opened – the owner came out. Instead of driving me away for occupying her doorway and disconcerting potential customers, she wished me well. The Tourist Office opened, and had bus timetables. Then I discovered I could go south rather than east, so rapidly booked for the next two nights. This meant buying a new map, as I'd stupidly cut off half of mine to save weight – a real false economy! Trudged through a cold drench from slobbering clouds, at ever-decreasing speed, to Tournon d'Agenais – 13km in two and a half hours. Wow! Arrived creaking. This route would miss all the touristy picturesque area, though I'd already seen Cahors, Cordes, and Albi; but it would also miss their prices and insufficient accommodation.

I was moving into a rolling secret countryside of woods and fields. All the streams were scads of foamy brown water; the Lot was in full spate. This road-walking was what I swore to avoid when I started, but the GR includes a lot of unclassified road, marked in white on the maps, which was acceptably empty. Departmental roads, usually yellow on the map, are a real pain for walkers though. **27km**

Day 59: I postponed the dread moment of setting off into the steady downpour by watching the tv weather forecast. Rain, though clearing, they said. There had been 65cm of snow in parts of the Pyrenees, and ramblers were being helicoptered out of mountain huts. I set off in the end, past a war-memorial to nine Resistance fighters: *'Aux victimes de l'ennemi de l'intérieur et l'extérieur'*, code for the Milice (French collaborators with the Gestapo) and the Germans. Without the physically challenging, direction-finding, waymark-spotting, decision-making skills of GR-walking, road-walking is a bore. And wet maize has low limits as a subject of speculation. Mentally I composed lists: birds I'd seen, birds I had expected to see but hadn't (rook, greenfinch), kit I'd carried all the way from Dieppe (sack, stick etc), departments I'd seen cars from, Italian towns beginning with B, things carried but never used (penknife, anti-diarrhoea pills, sleeping-bag), those things that the French do better than we do: markets, trains, taps (the new designs), wc flushes, elections, nursery schools, local pride, formal politeness, children's courts, celebrations, protest, Médecins Sans Frontières, inventiveness, screwcaps for beer-bottles, workers' participation, cheese, holidays, salad, postage stamps, support for remote villages, national pride, the range of their magazines, enjoying their children, living longer, postcodes . . . Inner resources were at a new low. I resisted the temptation to count my steps, though. A brown haze, a hangover scum on the mind, boredom coats one's awareness, which constantly needs reality's sandpaper. I often caught myself at a sort of toneless whistling based on Sibelius, punctuated by breathing in or out, by panting and, yes, by sighing.

A village cat (who says the beasts are intelligent?) spotted a moderately-paced car, jumped in front of it, hit the underside with a very audible thump, but darted off into bushes. A girl stopped to ask the way – it was not so much that I looked knowledgeable or trustworthy as that I was the only human visible for hundreds of miles. She was the fifth driver to do this, and the second I was able to help – don't motorists carry maps, then? I stopped to check my map and nibble chocolate on the cemetery steps.

The valley narrowed. Two fields, then one, was the width of civilisation. The woods closed in, dark, feral. Then, out on top, it was a decayed limestone plateau, small oaks, no more chestnuts. Rain prevented outdoor sitting-down, and there was nowhere to sit anyway, so I plodded straight on. Road-walking is kind on knees if not on hips, and you keep your feet dry. The whole countryside was under water at the moment – two ducks in a beanfield, turbid streamlets ferrying woody debris. Hotel (*'son tennis, son golf'*), and how nice to find words that are the same in both languages! As Henriette Walter, the linguist, has said: 'Our languages have had a relationship so durable and intimate that one can follow, in their vocabularies, the story of a long love-affair'; though sometimes it resembles even more closely the slightly exasperated interdependence of an old married couple. So we've taken, as well as *hotel* and *tennis*, and to give only a few of the most obvious: *café, bouquet* (both senses), *boutique, courier, ballet, chargé d'affaires, parquet.* And they, as well as *golf* and *tennis, WC, le white-spirit, le fair-play, stop* (and *non-stop*), *le patchwork, le crumble, le pack.* Sometimes they come out slightly wrong – *usherette, un job, foyer, un brushing* are not easily recognisable to their originators. And occasionally, they're so wrong you think it's on purpose: *le talkie-walkie, le shake-hand.* But there, once the words have got away, you're powerless to control them. Be proud of them having had the idea first.

Out after rest, into Montcuq, and found a bar/cheap hotel I didn't know about. Why wasn't it in the brochures? I was served hot chocolate by a perfunctory young man who went to talk with a young couple. The girl's mother came in, and with calm, relentless and indiscreet reasonableness criticised his behaviour until he said: 'I can take my car and leave.' And a minute later, he did so. An unrelated friend went with him. Mother cornered the girl behind counter and continued her remorseless, unwearying tirade; preventing the other person replying is itself a point made. A middle-aged couple came in for a drink but left swiftly when they realised what was going on. I left too, glad not to be staying there. Weather lifted for evening sun. Duck at dinner, with steak-knives. Don't they give the wrong message – 'We're going to serve some really tough meat: you'll need this'? **21km**

Day 60: I was last down for breakfast – that didn't happen very often. The weather had improved and I was pushed on by stiffish north-west wind, chill but clammy. Woodlarks just as in October; they don't have the breathcatching endlessness of skylarks, but delta-plane across the sky giving unimaginably varied changes on a five-to-seven note basic phrase. I practised baton-twirling and balancing – a new recreational use for the stick – though I had to give up when a fine, majorettish twirl landed the stick in the path of an oncoming car. Montcuq turned out to have several bars, open shops (though it was a bank holiday), a third hotel recycled as 'Bed and Breakfast' (sic). This is the GR 65, Le Puy to Roncesvaux, the way to Compostela, best-known and most used of all mediaeval pilgrimage routes. Every year 5,000 French pilgrims go, and many others too. Today the GR has three *topoguide*s of its own, and has become a fashionable walk even for non-pilgrims. I stood about a bit hoping to hear snatches from *Tannhäuser*, but soon realised that with my hat and staff I should be in a different opera, as Wotan the Wanderer. At last the grass was dry enough for me to lie down for lunch (choc and water). Found a jay's blue wing-feather for Huguette (that makes three or four). Took various wrong 'short-cuts', was barked at by various curs, nevertheless dawdled pleasurably through this self-contained, rolling, green countryside. Travelling through France is reading a book, field by field, wood by wood, stone by stone. Drivers zip by like diagonal speed-readers; I spell out every word like an open-mouthed child.

Several of the road-signs had recently been sprayed with the letters OC. This was the Languedoc word for 'yes', and is a political protest against Paris, for regional autonomy. Despite the official position of France as a single indivisible entity, there are plenty of regional claims for more independence. Supporters of this one confine themselves to spraying road-signs, but others, such as the Basques and the Bretons, sometimes go further on the road to terrorism. The overseas territories have independence movements. And the Corsicans are notorious for blowing up police stations and law-courts, and shooting political opponents and *préfets.* Moves by the present government to negotiate with the Corsican *indépendantistes* have horrified much of French public opinion. 'The children might have to learn Corsican, a dialect fit only for shepherds!. This conveniently ignores Alsace, where, without any fuss at all, the local dialect is tolerated, priests are paid by the State, ie by other French taxpayers, many of them not Christians, religious education is compulsory (everywhere else in French state schools it's banned), public holidays are different, the trains drive on the right just as they did when Alsace was ruled by Germany (except, apparently for the Paris–Mulhouse express, which keeps to the left. How they timetable this passes all understanding). Most French people don't know this example of their own multiculturalism.

But the cumulus was now acquiring dismayingly sharp edges, so I pressed on to Castelnau-Montratier. The indomitable Mrs Acland-Troyte, whose first name I would not presume to use even if I knew it, described it: 'On every side, save one, the steep rocky sides of the headland on which the town stands, form a natural fortification, which in case of invasion gives every advantage to the defending side; enabling the inhabitants to concentrate their forces and hold the enemy in check, along the narrow ridge which joins the peninsula to the plains behind, and is the one accessible side. But advantageous though the position of Castelnau, and all other similarly placed buildings may be by reason of their inaccessibility, this same inaccessibility is far from welcome to peaceful visitors who find themselves describing a cork-screw or spiral-like figure, in order to attain their destination; and so long after we saw Castelnau apparently within a stone's throw, we were still toiling along under the southern sun and following the vagaries of the twisting and twining white chalky way, which at last brought us to the neck of the peninsula, and so on into the little town.'

My path, clearly the one used by the locals to reach their fields, approached the town gate in an almost straight line. There were three windmills, one still with sails, an arcaded central square, only one letter-box, and one phone-booth (out of order). Swallows were nesting above café tables, six orange gapes whenever the parents arrived with food. The barmaid was justly proud, showed them off to the waitress at next café, who had chased hers away for fear of mess. As I watched, the first nestling left the nest, was actually airborne at one moment, perched on wire a couple of feet away. This precocious adventurousness was rewarded by the parents completely ignoring it, and after ten minutes it regained the warm, cosy, and catered-for nest. Old men passed, still wearing blue as a reminder of their working days; women swept the pavement in front of the door; little PO vans went by. Vigorous men in their fifties, with high stomachs under T-shirts advertising American colleges, and with very short shorts and espadrilles, strolled round the square; they carried leather purses with wrist-thongs. Washed feet and socks in bidet (and why do they always wobble? Bidet stories on a postcard, please). At the Maison de Retraite with a picture-window on to the street, the old people had been unimaginatively seated in rows facing each other, so that half of them couldn't see what was going on outside, and were straining ageing necks to keep up with life. Monument in the main square to the Immaculate Conception, or rather to the Pope's proclamation of it in 1854; it was adorned with plaques to the locally-born great and good of the Church. **19km**

Day 61: Market! Monthly, so there was serious stuff. Wallpaper, rather frumpy clothes for both sexes, shoes, hats, belts, jewellery and other accessories, flowers (slow-burn geraniums, natty pansies), seeds, kitchen equipment, no fruit or veg. Gradually the dark-grey clouds turned to white, the paler bits to blue, then it was fair-weather cumulus and hot sun. By the end of the afternoon I was done *à point*, with lightly-crisped scalp. A shuttered house in Auty had a peacock sitting on the verandah rail, but it wouldn't open its tail, even though I gave my best imitation of a rival peacock, alarming the dogs for 100m in every direction.

For two days now I'd been crossing rivers (and roads in the valleys) running north-east to south-west. It was all up and down as I crossed the Boudouyssou, Séoune, Petite Barguelonne, Barguelonne, Lendou, Lembous, Lupte, Lemboulas, Petit Lembous, Lère. Funny to think that all French rivers preserve their pre-Roman Celtic names, and many (eg Seine, Dordogne) their pre-Celtic names from well before 500BC and perhaps back to Cro-Magnon times. What must have meant 'stream', 'the flooder', 'the source of life', or 'our river' in some pre-Celtic tongue has survived to be simply an opaque proper name, like those above.

Cheap hotel in Caussade, the sort where you pay in advance and the fluorescent tube above the washbasin has been nicked. Someone tried my doorhandle twice. I arranged my stick as wedge and alarm. Bought total block in chemist's – still open after 6pm – a belatedly sensible move, as my head was tingling and sore, and they were announcing a real heatwave for the weekend. Rain and melting snow had caused severe flooding further south. Then I sat in the evening sun outside, while the locals came and went. Meal excellent – copious, tasty, cheap. Other guests included two workers at local factory, boarding by the week, and three younger men looking for work. Four went to bed early, only a middle-aged Spaniard and I watched the Slovenia v Yugoslavia football match. **22.5km**

Day 62: Uneventful night. The three job-seekers set off early with holdalls slung round their necks with cord. I was on a luxury trip, compared. Phoned *chambre d'hôte* for weekend. Three were already full, but the fourth had room. 'No evening meal, though,' he warned me, so I told him 'Fine, I'll eat at midday or bring a picnic as I'm on foot.' 'On foot!' he exclaimed, 'no problem then, we'll find you something to eat.' The total block was marvellous. I smeared it on at 8am and by midday the sun still hadn't broken through the mist. Long (12km) and very boring road to start with, then 5km on minor road between cliffs and the heavily and noisily swollen Aveyron brought me to Bruniquel, a fortified village and château perched on what looked like a perfectly inaccessible rock-spur. But despite steepness, the path went up through little twisty cobbled streets, houses with red geraniums everywhere and not a soul to be seen except British tourists in the bar. Once again the phone box was out of order.

After salad and a beer for lunch, I followed the GR 46 along some very pretty minor roads, through a hamlet called Brian de Vère, a suitable mate for the Sylve d'Argençon of Day 41, then up an endless stony slope in full sun. What shade there was was already occupied by an astonishing variety of prickly plants. Sweating profusely, and stopping for breath every hundred metres, I reached the top, passed ruined barns and a deserted hamlet, then stumbled down other side in thick mud and more prickly plants, struggled across flooded streams on fallen trees, swore I'd take the next metalled road, chickened out when I found it was twice the distance. Nasty surprise when I suddenly saw that my right shoe, which had been suffering from a slight hernia, had sprung a fully-formed tramp-like gape between sole and upper. After only 1500km! And just as my feet had got used to them! They weren't cheap either, and supposedly designed for this sort of walking. Huh! This was the first section where I'd not had serious problems with blisters. I improvised a closure with a spare lace.

I met two French walkers with IGN map, out for the afternoon, older than I, but very keen, and was able to direct them to the isolated chapel they were looking for. Last three kilometres had a total *dénivelé* of 400m, an average gradient of one in seven-and-a-half. Finally I stormed the fortified hill-top village of Puycelsi (aka Puycelci) where, despite it being Monday, one of the two bars was open. I drank two shandies to bring me back from the dead, an increasingly frequent need. Three young people arrived in minibus with ten mentally-handicapped kids – seating them in café, ordering drinks, keeping them entertained and acceptable, taking them out of sight to pee – they're heroes really.

Down the hill to *chambre d'hôte*, where Mme Gaignard, who had been running *chambres d'hôte* for twenty-two years, and had done some walking herself, took one look at my face and gave me a drink, then questioned me closely about my route. So I'd seen a family and two children in that isolated hour, had I? It must be one advantage of being on foot that you acquire a knowledge of the country that flatters locals, by enabling discussion of ruined farmhouses, restored barns etc that are an integral part of their lives. You can give information as well as receive it. We ate out on the terrace in the evening sun with the other guest, a Parisian walker, who'd been doing the Gorges of the Tarn, from the source to Albi, not a bad idea at all, and was now winding down in this area. He talked of his doings rather than himself, and was overly keen on approving of the 'right' things – Roquefort, Najac, Scotland, French cooking. Deference diffused is difference defused. But I'm addicted to difference, and provocatively pressed the claims of Chinese and Turkish cuisine (not to the detriment of the French, of course). He was silently amazed when Mme and I agreed on how disappointing we'd found the Château de Chambord. 'Such a lump!' 'And that terrible roof!' A storm cloud a few miles away turned out later to have been dropping 4cm of rain in an hour on Albi, but we enjoyed a serene dusk. **29km**

Day 63: The mist was already melting at 8am – the promised heat-wave was coming. Mme Gaignard let me use her phone to try for tonight's accommodation, but the hotel I had been counting on was closed for pre-season refurbishment, and the *chambres d'hôte* were poorly placed for walkers, so it would be Gaillac for tonight, and a really long day on Sunday. Small roads were very pleasant in the mid-morning cool,

My jury-rigged lace was still holding the shoe together, but there was little pleasure left in the act of walking, more in the progress than the means of progression. It was a butterfly day; a Large Tortoiseshell settled on my shirt – could it be my sweet blossom-like nature that attracted them? Then I saw five on a deer turd. White Admirals everywhere, then what must be a Purple Emperor.

I met a woman looking for fungi in the forest. Then, once again found that following the waymarks had brought me somewhere I didn't expect. So a long slog along the main road dreaming of cooler autumn, the 'hammer of heat' made just bearable by breeze and one or two cloudlets. I knew I'd never feel cool again. First cicadas. Coaches passed, their tinted windows making all the occupants look Asiatic; conversely, they saw all the bright countryside dulled and distant, as if on a screen. Waved to, and was waved to by *vignerons* among the vines. Women in flowered aprons over dark grey frocks, and in battered broad-brimmed straw hats were working in the vineyards too. Their mothers would have been all in black, their daughters will be in jeans, and their grand-daughters in bikinis very likely. I'll be back.

The wines of Gaillac, like many of those of South and South-West France, have been undergoing a renaissance recently. Despite being one of the oldest wine areas in France (in the tenth century the monks were already legislating to protect its reputation), and very popular in Victorian England, Gaillac's wines fell on hard times in the twentieth century. Only a disciplined programme of weeding out old vines and mentalities has started their revival of the last twenty years. Usual problems with hotels on spec; the first advertised rooms by the hour, too like a *boui-boui* (knocking-shop), not a brothel, where the 'girls' are resident, but a *maison de passe*, where you bring your own partner and pay by the hour. The next one was shut. The third sounded very posh, but was OK really – clean, central, cheapish. Somewhere today I crossed another frontier. For the first time on the whole walk, and for the remainder of it, I was in a part of France never subject to an English monarch (Saunur town was an exception).

I visited the town park in the late afternoon, by a small neat brick château on a terrace above the Tarn. There were shady walks under plane trees and horse-chestnuts, pools running into one another, lawns, fountains, girl joggers, mothers with pushchairs. Fountains are an art in southern countries, the play of light and sound contributing to the coolness. In Britain, they're just another reminder of rain. These gardens were designed by Le Nôtre, who did the ones at Versailles.

But it was dismaying how it had all started to drag now that I was in the beloved Midi. Perhaps I should have done it in reverse, so as to get the novelty at the end? But then what would have been perfect? And perhaps fatigue was partly to blame. Walking and heat and the weight of the sack tire of course, but it's loneliness that puts the real strain on inner resources. Out to Chinese restaurant (always worth a try in France) and was attacked by sharp twinge, like a seriously severe tickle, in right hip. Oh, no! This couldn't be last year's problem recurring, surely? It wasn't quite in the same place, and movement calmed it, but no still position was pain free, and it was accompanied by cramps in both hands. Woke in the night to a second attack, took more steroids and painkillers, lay awake making plans to abort this chunk of the trip as I had the first. Was I ever going to be able to complete? **24.5km**

Day 64: At 8am, no pain in hip! Deciding it might have been a result of yesterday's desiccation, I'd go as far as Graulhet, which is big enough to have a bus service to Albi or Toulouse, and see what happened. Breakfast on *terrasse* in sun and shade. From open windows of flats all round, women were shaking dusters and chatting. Thin elegant girls with short hair, neat necks and thick-soled trainers, clumped along the streets to college.

Brens, the first village on my route, was the site of an internment camp during World War II. Its twenty wooden huts were constructed for 1000 Belgian refugees who had fled into France before the invading Wehrmacht. They went home after the Armistice of June 1940, and the camp was used to shelter destitute foreign Jews. Up to 1,200 lived there in reasonably good conditions. There was a school for the children, religious practices could be correctly observed, inmates were allowed out into the village and even to Gaillac. But the anti-Jewish legislation of the Vichy government meant they were moved to more 'secure' accommodation early in 1941. The third group to be imprisoned here was several hundred women, many of them political prisoners, like those in Fanlac (Day 53), but others were petty criminals and prostitutes, and a group of Spanish refugees with their children, whom the authorities had no idea how else to deal with. Jews among them were deported to German concentration camps. This was only one camp of many such.

In June 1944 the remaining prisoners were sent to the notorious camp of Gurs, in the Pyrenées Atlantiques. Nice to report that they were so disgusted by the conditions in their new quarters that they set fire to it, and threatened to burn the whole camp. Clearly internment hadn't broken their spirit. A pity I learnt about all this only later, or I would have paid more attention at the time.

Across rich farmland, cereals with some vines, pale gold wheat and pale copper barley. New houses everywhere, all occupied; three cars outside was quite usual, this isn't *résidence secondaire* (holiday home) country. Some of the inhabitants must have been retired, but others were the local farmers, and some were commuters, perhaps to Toulouse, barely an hour's drive away. The landscape was rolling, with numerous knolls, many with woods on top, some with farmhouses (where did they get water?), some with both. At Labessière-Candeil, it was the village fête this weekend: street-party, competitions for fishing, *pétanque, belote*, three dances (one disco, two with that emblem of *la France profonde*, the accordion). Most of the public space of the village was occupied by a traditional fair, with dodgems, hoopla, shooting galleries, merry-go-rounds. The village had provided decorative street-lights. Two gypsy-ish girls were laying out the prizes – teddy-bears, tinsel, foil balloons etc. Their mother and a boy were cleaning out the public toilets – not up to their standard.

All over France, banners – '*Grandes fêtes de*______', or '_____ *en fête*' – come out on roads and bridges; flags go up along the streets, stages are erected for the bands. Originally on the fête of the church's patron saint, most are now put on in July and August, or at weekends, to attract a maximum of holiday-makers.

Competitions are organised, as at Labessière-Candeil, but tennis, volleyball, clay pigeon shooting(*le ball-trap*) as well. Torchlight processions, folk-dancing, picnics, firework displays, cycle or foot races, games for children, talent competitions, Mass, a speech by M le Maire - often at the war-memorial; bars on the square, pancakes, *merguez* (spicy sausages, North African in origin), popcorn, confetti, bangers of both sorts, party-poppers, candy-floss. There may be a pony-show or an exhibition of a rural craft – clog-making, sheep-shearing, logging, bell-ringing – though I've never seen the sort of thing so popular in England like jam-making and giant leek competitions, flower shows, egg-and-spoon races. After the speeches there may be a *vin d'honneur*, free drinks offered by the organisers on the village square, sometimes an *apéritif dansant*. Almost everyone dances: married couples, parents with little children clasped round their necks, two women together (why don't men dance?). Many people return to 'their' village for the occcasion, so it's a time for renewing old acquaintances. The colour, music, high spirits show that despite it all, there's still hope for the human race.

Ready for the fête

'In the centre of the square, erect a pole wreathed in flowers; gather the people together, and you've a fête'. Rousseau again, who looked like being one of the guardian angels of my enterprise. Here he's contrasting the theatre (a small number of people, silent, in the dark, passive, separate, being communicated at; the stage equals the monarchy), with fêtes (collective, democratic, active, visible), whose only purpose is to show the participants off to each other. Even Rousseau, though, sees 'the people' as needing someone to set up the maypole for them, and call them together. '*Comités des Fêtes*' for exactly this purpose, are volunteered for the occasion, usually with subsidies from the municipality (there are 30,000 of these in France, so the total expense is considerable).

So to Graulhet, which is a leather town. The inhabitants pronounce it Gro-lay, curiously, as if it were *gros* (big) and *laid* (ugly). But to north and south it is known as Gro-yay (as the spelling should imply). The leather is sheepskin, morocco, pigskin, for every purpose except shoes. Not much in evidence, by the smell for example.

Large, or at least prominent, North African population. The men

Almost everyone dances

were sitting at the PMU café, neither betting nor drinking alcohol. Both French and Arabic were being spoken. Muslim girls were going home from school, and a very striking spectacle they made, with Euro-fashionable stretch trousers, bare arms even; head-coverings, however minimal, such as scrunchies, or butterfly-clips, were the give-away. The breeze quickened as the heat declined and the shade spread. Someone came in wanting to know how to reach a certain street; six men spilled on to the pavement to point out the best way – at least three versions were favoured. He drove off, ignored, while they continued to argue the pros and cons of the suggested routes.

Old men in vests and white shorts watched the *pétanqueurs*, with even older men in shirts, braces and caps. The centre of the square still reverberated with the day's stored heat. A stage had been set up, with thirty or forty chairs in front. Suddenly a concert started. *La Fanfare Graulhétoise*. Wow! Especially the massed sousaphones! There were forty young but enthusiastic players, their inexperience stiffened by half-a-dozen older players. Eight of the ten percussionists were girls, and they were good! The percussion section had won a national award the week before.

Their parents applauded; their friends, who had come to scoff, remained to cheer. What a fine way to end the day, a community gathering in the cool of the oncoming dusk. But what would Rousseau have made of this? **23km**

Day 65: No further hip problem, and a short day ahead. I lay in for an hour, storing as much of the coolness as possible, against the heat of the day. The hotel manager regretted her lack of time to enjoy the countryside: she used to cycle everywhere, and wanted to know the details of my route. Much high thin cloud about – yesterday had been pure blue – announcing wind and giving some cover.

Agreeable lanes out of town to a countryside like yesterday's, with more forest southwards. A pack of four dogs raved at me – a woman emerged from the house – I asked whether she enjoyed the racket. She shut the beasts up, apologising; I thanked her. Why can't it always be like this?

On to the ridge-top and, suddenly through a gap in the trees, saw the low black line of the Montagne Noire to the south-east, and then, with snow on their upper slopes, the Pyrenees, from the Carlit, due south, to the Mont Valier, south-west; with all my mountains – Aspre, Endron dominating Goulier my final destination, Malcarras, Médécourbe, Soucarrane, Canalbonne, Montcalm, Brougat, and all the rest – clustered in the middle. It was too far to recognise each one, but I knew it was them, so broke into song:

Aquelos montanyos que tant hautos son
M'empechan di beire mas amos on son.

(These mountains that are so high
Prevent me seeing where my love doth lie.)

Supposedly by Gaston Phébus, fourteenth century Count of Foix, this song is pretty well the anthem of the Ariège Pyrenees. Five kilometres into Brousse in hopes of a bar. Dashed. So I tramped 6.5km along the busy road to Lautrec, where I arrived feeling as if my legs were worn down to the length of the artist's. Lautrec is yet another mediaeval fortified town on a hill-top, with mediaeval houses, a seventeenth century windmill restored in 1991, potters everywhere, along with painters, wrought-iron makers etc. Two eight-year-olds, sniggering as they plucked up courage, asked me, 'Walking's good for you, isn't it?' The same thing had happened on Day 9! This must be some catch phrase, probably from a children's tv programme or advert. But intensive questioning among my acquaintances of the right age has not revealed the source.

More fêtes were advertised, with curiously-named bands: Poupou's Swing, Silly Laughing Sods, If You See Kay. What? Oh, IC! Why does 'fuck' attract non-native speakers so much? *Fucking Amal* is a Swedish film, 'fcuk' is an international clothing and accessories company, 'Fuck Police' say graffiti in Croatia, where only British tourists can understand, though Croatian police probably have a shrewd idea.

Don't these people have taboo words of their own? No, is the answer I'm afraid. English is unique in its social, magic power to shock. That's why it's best for poetry. And why is it only in their transferred, offensive, sense that these words are used? It's quite common to see them printed, even in daily newspapers. But in their true senses? Never! It would be a pity if indigenous illiterates, American politicians, and sensation-seeking foreigners took that away. Join HOOT: Hands Off Our Taboos!

Really hot (32°C, 90°F) when I left Lautrec at 3.30pm, fortified by, if weighed down with, two litres of St Yorre. Lost my way slightly trying a short-cut down a small lane, which ended in a rural farmyard, earth with a few rocks jutting here and there; hens were pecking desultorily in the shade, watched with feigned interest by a cat. Curtains covered the doorways, flapping lazily; pots of geraniums stood on the windowsills; a great pile of rusting agricultural machinery lay under a hawthorn bush.

No one responded to my presence, so I beat a retreat to the last crossroads, where I upset two people in a cottage by lying on a lane-side verge in the shade. 'Is that chap still there?' called the husband. 'Yes, dammit!' Plodded gamely on, amid scents of broom, tar and dry grass, to Puycalvel and the *chambre d'hôte*, where I was warmly welcomed by Mme Arcambal. Did I mind that there was a cot in the same room? Would I like to use the swimming-pool? No trunks, I regretted. Regretted it still more when through the shutters I saw a topless young woman sun-creaming her breasts by the said pool. I had thought of bringing trunks, naturally. The mere thought of slipping into cool water after a hot 20km....Aaah! But only a fool would have swum in the obviously polluted water of the Orne below Caen, or the Seine near its mouth. And common sense wasn't enough. On a hydrographic map of France, with the quality of river water graded on a five-point scale, there was nowhere before the Pyrenees where I would come across 'excellent' and a dismayingly large number of 'very bad' – chromium from tanneries and fell-mongering at Graulhet, for example; waste from the slaughterhouses at Parthenay; widespread agricultural nitrate and slurry pollution, and simple failure by large towns to treat their sewage. Even the picturesque Dordogne, Lot and Tarn, their banks thronged with happy campers, rarely reach 'good'.

Visited the village; there was a '*café*', which turned out to be pretty well the grocer's front room. Over a beer, we discussed English families in the village, the weather, the *vent d'autan* (a local hot strong wind);

she quoted a proverb in patois to the effect that if it blew on Palm Sunday it would blow for the rest of the year. It had done. Round here it was violent, though Revel, my next stop, was agreed to be the windiest place. Must support these tiny commercial ventures that keep the villages socially afloat. She, like Mme Arcambal, rolled her 'r' Scots-fashion, not at all like the guttural French 'r'. This is normal, if socially suspect, from here southwards.

Over the promised dinner, outside on the terrace, with the Arcambals and a couple of regular guests from Ille-et-Vilaine in the north, conversation ranged widely and included the British Royal Family (they knew all their ages; I didn't). The Ille-et-Vilaine couple lived quite near where Caroline Dickinson was murdered in a hostel dormitory – nobody had yet been caught. We discussed genetic fingerprinting, capital punishment, police inefficiency; then Anglicanism, hunting, nicknames. What I had thought to be early onions in the fields was declared to be huge garlic. Lautrec is the centre for pink garlic, famed for its taste and stamina compared to the less aristocratic violet variety.

Apparently several nearby farms had been bought by farmers coming from the Sarthe, round Le Mans, which may help explain why I had seen so many deserted farms there in October. M Arcambal was using an Opinel knife to cut and eat his meal, though rather secretive about it in company. Meanwhile two Green Woodpeckers, a Little Egret, a rabbit, a Sparrowhawk, and a Golden Oriole passed, and a peacock called from the neighbouring farm. M Arcambal invited me to watch the second half of England v Germany (1–0). I got very excited, but it might as well have been San Marino v Moldova for him – rightly, as it turned out, when neither England nor Germany survived the first round, and France won the title. **21km**

Day 66: Night interrupted by dogs, wind, nightingales, peacock. Bell rang for the monthly mass, in the morning – Madame might be going, Monsieur definitely not. 'The church won't fall on him,' she said with fond asperity. What were definitely Cattle Egrets in field with cows – could some of yesterday's little egrets have been these? Not all, I decided, consulting my notes. Passed a war memorial to a doctor, shot by the Resistance in July 1944 '*par méprise*', by mistake; they took him for a collaborator or Nazi sympathiser, and he wasn't. It's been calculated that in the *épuration* (clearing-up) of 1944-45, about 9,000 people were executed summarily, and 900 after a trial of some sort. Women supposed to have slept with German soldiers had their heads shaved in public – how many is not known, of course. When will the full story of these post-war revenges be told? In the bigger villages everyone was buying *pâtisseries* before going to see granny for Sunday meal. Sat on bridge in shade, and knocked my stick into the stream; could NOT do without it; though great ingenuity and equilibrium were needed to retrieve it.

Into Puylaurens, yet another hill-top town. For centuries it has been the centre of the cultivation of *pastel* (woad), now grown as cattle fodder rather than for its blue dye. As far as I know, the ancient Gauls didn't use it as facial war-paint as the ancient Britons did. Yesterday's almost *Pilgrim's Progress* vision of the Pyrenees was today obscured by heat haze. The war memorial in Puylaurens had soldiers listed by rank, first officers, then men (oh dear!); usually it's by date or alphabetical order. The French are always surprised to learn the number of British and Commonwealth citizens killed in France in World War I (more than half a million from the UK). There's a low-level but persistent belief that no British soldiers fought in France in 1914-18 though nobody who lives near the great British cemeteries of the Somme and north-east France subscribes to this. Of course, the French lost many more, approximately twice as many – figures which have served politicians in subsequent debacles. But take your French friends round a village war memorial or two in the UK; they'll be surprised just as my mother-in-law was. 'They never told us this!' she exclaimed at the number of dead. Your friends may also ask why we don't keep our memorials in better nick. But then they don't have poppies or a two minute silence for remembering.

As I was sitting in the bar having yet another double shandy (only a week ago it had been hot chocolate) there passed huge vans advertising the US Postal Service, Banesto, Cofidis, la Française des Jeux. These are support vehicles for the professional cycling teams. Suddenly I remembered there was a race, the *Route du Sud*, finishing nearby that

A multi-coloured toneless whoosh

afternoon – was it coming through here? Especially as I was wearing my 'Tour de France in Brighton' T-shirt again. Quick search of paper, though, showed I was out of luck. It would pass where I was yesterday. Later this year, for the third time in its history, the Tour itself ends a stage in Revel, where I'm now headed. (PS – when it did come, David Millar of Scotland came fourth. Hurrah!) On July 11, unfortunately. I've seen the tour twice – it's breathtaking. The few seconds it takes to pass are unforgettable, a multi-coloured toneless whoosh as all those spokes slice through the startled air.

I should have guessed from the lack of crowds that this was not the place to see a cycle race. The Tour is another component of *la France profonde* – it draws bigger crowds than any other sporting event in the world. It's a thousand-mile long *fête*. Full of *convivialité*, the French line the route, picnicking while they wait. There's no yobbishness, no streaking, no fighting, no conspicuous drunkenness, no racist chanting, an infinitesimal role for political protest. Just millions of people clapping and cheering the human achievement. And it's free.

The afternoon, long, as expected, started OK; the way went along the main road, past one of those villages that tourists go through without stopping on the way to somewhere else, are through before they know they've arrived, indeed. In this case with justification. Then it produced 5km of the most disagreeable walking since Dieppe. The wind, the famous *vent d'autan*, was now gusting up to raging-gale force, and the road went through a plane tree avenue. These were originally planted to give shade to Napoleon's infantry, but by now have become a real menace. I lurched between verge and tarmac, sometimes simply sheltering behind a tree till the wind died down a bit. Branches, leaves and twiglets pattered down, including three biggish ones. Drivers stopped for these, and swerved round. Cursing myself for a big softy, I flicked them into the ditch . Life is so temporary for drivers – they could have done this for themselves, but hey! 'I'm past, sod the others'. Within mere seconds they're miles away. Tired and fed up, I dodged from tree to tree, impatient to be back home.

Would I ever have made it this far in a single go, as planned? Probably I'd have cracked psychologically if my hip hadn't gone first. Solitude, which I can bear, was on the verge of becoming loneliness. There would undoubtedly have been problems of accommodation, as this year, but they would have been far worse in July and August. And it would have been much longer – by not sticking to the GR 36 I'd cut 250km off the original itinerary. The wind blew agreeably enough up the legs of my shorts, but disagreeably into my eyes; several times it took my hat off. Finally I struggled as far as Revel and my hotel. Bath and leg inspection – the wounds inflicted by the fallen trees a fortnight ago had at last healed; just a few scars down my left shin to enhance the two already in residence.

Like Monpazier, Revel is a bastide, founded by the French though, in 1332. The classically-arcaded central square has a truly enormous covered market. There is plenty of evidence of Revel's industries – furniture-making and mint liqueur. In the town were at least two other walkers wandering round; one in sandals with badly packed sack, tent dangling at angle, weight far back for maximum leverage, the other with stick and high pack, but drifting as if in a dream. There was a curious shame-faced air of defeat about both of them. Even the young men in Caussade looking for work seemed more cheerful, optimistic, better armed against fate. Are we walkers such wimps, then?

I'd arranged to meet my soon-to-be-ex-brother-in-law, but there was no sign. As soon as I sat down at table, though, he joined me, with his new partner. They'd been cycling in the Montagne Noire nearby. A pleasant evening. I'd not seen him for nearly two years; we did some excellent walks together in the Pyrenees, before troubles blew up. Naturally, we talked of everything except those troubles, though I did make sure if he was still in touch with his children. **30km**

Day 67: The wind died down in the night, but by 9am was rising to yesterday's strength. The path led uphill to the Bassin de St Ferréol and across the dam in a howling gale. This dam dates from 1666, when Paul Riquet decided to construct a canal to link Atlantic and Mediterranean. Others had had this idea before, but what defeated them was the water-supply. Canals need to be fed at the top. The Seuil de Naurouze, the watershed between the Atlantic and the Mediterranean, and the gap between the Montagne Noire and the foothills of the Pyrenees, is not steep, nor exceptionally high (194m), but it doesn't have an obvious water-supply. Riquet built three artificial lakes in the Montagne Noire, of which St Ferréol is the biggest, to give a constant supply of water at the needed point. Canalisations are everywhere, all beautifully engineered at a constant gradient. Riquet died, hugely in debt, six months before the Canal du Midi was opened in 1681. These days, there's little or no commercial traffic, but it's a popular cruise, despite the 103 locks, from Toulouse to the Etang de Thau, near Sète. St Ferréol is popular for outdoor activities: a school of canoeists was getting launched; on the other side of the path twenty or so cyclists were following the *rigole*, the water supply channel. I moved to one side and was nearly knocked down by a herd of joggers.

Up the hillside, where a surreally optimistic man asked if I might possibly be carrying a screwdriver – he'd locked himself out of his car. Could this be the first opportunity to use my penknife? No, the blade was far too short. The highest point so far (620m), and over the watershed into the Mediterranean basin. Yet another frontier.

The top is grass and cereal land, and also mobile aerial land, I was sorry to see; at one point there were more than twenty in sight. Despite considerable gaps, due to its extent (it's twice the area of the UK, and more than four times that of England) and considerably rougher relief, France has taken to mobiles with the same enthusiasm as we have: '*Chérie, je suis dans le train*'. Public kiosks are less and less used; indeed, rural areas will pass straight from coin-operated phones to mobiles, without passing through the card stage at all. Kiosks will atrophy, like public clocks and public transport. The French do trust technology, though. They talk at normal volume into their mobiles, not like the Brits, who secretly believe it must need help, and bellow. The 1,000ft climb in shady woodland had been no problem, but now the descent in suffocating shadeless loops made me glad I wasn't going in the other direction.

So I'd try the final section in the autumn. Last October's walk had been a real success. And this decision led to yet another discovery about why I was doing this – the need to produce order out of chaos demands a steady supply of chaos; disorder your life so as to reshape its patterns again.

One of a set of plastic roadside bollards was infested with snails. At the top was a small thicket of the small pointed ones; then perhaps eighty ordinary striped ones grouped around, with others still climbing up. None of the other bollards had a single one. No doubt a long-advertised snail orgy, or rave.

The bar in St Papoul was closed on Mondays, a pretty young woman informed me. Guess what day it was? It seems to have replaced Sunday as the day of rest in France. So I tackled 9km of rather too main road into Castelnaudary, at long last getting some helpful backing from the wind. A long series of Army vehicles, with drivers under instruction, caused unpredictable risks. Cars zipped past, one driven by a terminally deaf rock-fan. I was crossing the plain of the Fresquel, an insignificant stream; this plain was the scene of the last great rebellion of the Midi against centralising Paris, in 1632, when the Governor of the Languedoc led a revolt against the annulling of the province's right to raise taxes. Of course, he lost; and was beheaded in Toulouse (where a plaque on the Capitole, the City Hall, commemorates the event).

Keats got it spectacularly wrong when he wrote:

There is a charm in footing slow across a silent plain,
Where patriot battle has been fought, where glory had the gain.

There may have been more charm in the walking in Scotland, but for most people here, it wasn't a matter of patriotism or glory, whether the taxes were raised by X or Y didn't make a penn'orth of difference.

I passed the big basin on the canal, and the ladder of locks. The SNCF station appeared to be an industrial wasteland, all dusty silos and four storeys of broken windows. Closer inspection revealed bar, hotels, other facilities. I booked a ticket to Dieppe for tomorrow, with a reduction for over-sixties, a reduction open to all Europeans.

In the hotel I removed the laces (re-usable) from my shoes before binning the wretched things. Then lay on the bed staring at the ceiling for an hour – the book I'd brought for this section, selected poems by Ben Jonson, had been useless; the good ones are well known and far too few, the others, especially the epigrams, are inexcusably dire. Then dinner, and sleep. **29km**

7

September – Castelnaudary to Goulier

Day 68: Huguette's sister, Suzy, drove us to Castelnaudary station, and we set off on the last section, up the Avenue Paul Riquet, and along the tow-path round the Grand Bassin of the Canal du Midi – little houses and gardens almost to the water's edge – we'd just room to get by. A fly, stupidly not looking where it was going, zoomed straight down Huguette's throat, from where no amount of coughing and cursing could retrieve it. Tactfully, I suppressed the classic remedy – 'swallow a spider'. A tight-lipped silence ensued nevertheless. Along the canal, there were lots of pleasure cruisers at every lock. In a fine display of techno-machismo the men were jumping about with coils of rope and cries of 'Hard a-starboard!' and 'Full steam ahead!', while the women treated the helm as though it were simply a steering-wheel, or sat knitting. It doesn't look a very exciting mode of travel. From water level , you could hardly see the countryside over the banks.

Even though it was Sunday, every lock was manned, all the cottages were inhabited, the keepers busy with the traditional sluice-key, but also with a mobile to the next colleague, with news of how many boats, and when. The work proceeded at a stately, almost cumbersome, rhythm; just as the distances between locks are advertised to the nearest metre, each second needed its due. About 4km from Castelnaudary, Fanjeaux, our evening's destination, came into sight on a prominent hill to the south-east. It's visible from miles around. No wonder eighteenth century geographers took the church tower as a triangulation point for their maps of France. Beyond the towpath it was shooting season; one man hidden in the undergrowth showed us his bag, a red-legged partridge, or Frenchie. The English ones were introduced from France. One road sign bore the traditional marks of hunting country – it was peppered with shot. Almost all rural signs used to show these scars; it was good to see that some traditions were still being maintained. You can see a similar thing in Mexico, though there the pattern of the holes shows that bullets, not shot, have been used....

By the Canal du Midi

We scrumped ripe walnuts behind a keeper's cottage. The newly-laid towpath surface was rough gravel, and very hard on the feet, so we were glad to get away after 12km. The path led through surprisingly bare countryside – all cereals, maize, sunflowers, millet etc had been harvested, leaving a landscape of ochre soil and grey stalks; only asparagus still showed green. Two more snail parties, one covering several square metres. The most enthusiastic had climbed several feet up a tree. There seems to be some connection with fennel, which also abounded at these spots. Where there was growth, it was fruit; as well as walnuts, we passed passion fruit, almonds, figs, grapes, apples, quinces, persimmons, pomegranates and others neither of us recognised. The track had been ploughed up at one point – the owner retains all his rights, just as in England – but a small boy pointed out the way, and we picked our way gingerly across, past groups of hunters, some boasting so loudly that there was no game within 100m. Arrived in Villasavary to find café closed so we plumped ourselves down on a bench, to be approached by a talkative and nosy old resident. He was most impressed to discover we were both teachers, spreading wide his hands to show how much brain we must have. He'd once walked to Mirepoix (*c*30km), when he was young, during the war. Now he did 6km a day. Villasavary, for all its lack of facilities, and it was Sunday after all, had ingeniously decorated its rubbish containers with primitive paintings of village scenes. Some people were visiting the *Mairie* to vote (always on a Sunday in France), on a change of Constitution. There was widespread apathy, it was no surprise to learn that it was only a thirty per cent turnout; but they can't change things any other way. Then last 4km to Fanjeaux, quite viciously uphill near the finish. There was an appalling mix-up at the *gîte* – all my fault – phoning in near darkness, I'd mixed the numbers. Angrily, I practically accused them of lying. But calm prevailed in the end. So we were not booked here, after all, and were booked somewhere else, but didn't know where. After some casting around, the somewhere else turned out to be the Dominican Convent. A nice Filipino sister greeted us, showed us to a simple, spotless, room. Dinner in the same vein, meatless. Nobody asked if we're married, or Catholics. We were even given a key, to allow us out in the evening. We made for the stunning view northwards in the late evening light. It was from here, in 1206, that St Dominic saw fire descend on a spot at the foot of the hill, where he founded another convent. The name Fanjeaux comes from the Latin *Fanum Jovis*, the Temple of Jupiter; I'd guess this was a holy place long before the Romans, too. Its prominent situation, and the fact that there appears to have been a pond on the actual summit would make an impression on anyone. A tense and silent struggle is taking place between the Dominicans and the tourist industry. Dominic's call was to preach against the local heretics, the Cathars, or Albigensians; he would have nothing to do with the Crusade which, using the heresy as an excuse, looted, pillaged, and massacred the rich Languedoc for more than thirty years. As well as the site of his vision and two convents, the village also contains a house where he used to stay, and a modern building for seminarians. But the tourist industry is focussed on the

Cathars. They lost, were killed or burnt or converted, so have all the romantic aura of mystery and gallant failure that makes Brits favour Cavaliers rather than Roundheads, and Scots side with Bonnie Prince Charlie. Everywhere we found paths marked *'Sentier des Cathares', 'Chemin des Cathares'*, castles referred to as *'château Cathare'*; all without a shred of historical evidence. To the Catholic Church, of course, they're still heretics. To the resulting sense of stress that we divined was added another; that between locals and incoming artists – potters, antique dealers, painters on one surface or another. Altogether an uneasy place. **24km**

Day 69: Simple breakfast at the acceptably worldly hour of 8.15am. Huguette was taken off to visit the chapel. I wrote in the visitors' book – compliments only, solitude is better for poetry-writing, whatever else it does to you. I was restored to company and silence, when the sister appeared, and the delicate question of cost arose. 'You can give something if you like,' she said under pressure. We calculated what B&B might have cost, and added a bit. Then out again into agricultural wilderness like yesterday's. One shepherdess looking for mushrooms; nice mixture of road, cart-track, foot-path. The path runs along the watershed between the Mediterranean on the left, and the Atlantic on the right, before deciding for the latter. In one corner of a field we found a cross, marking a death at the spot in 1882. There was a fine view over miles of sunlit hills; when you've got to go, you could do a great deal worse than somewhere like this.

At Hounoux a large number of Belgian-registered cars showed how many of these small, isolated villages are becoming holiday destinations for Northerners. Suddenly, an owl leered at us from a roadside tree, only a couple of metres away. It leant drunkenly to one side; its eyes were yellow glass, and it had a festive straw on its head. If it had been able to giggle, it would have. Brussels must be a riot. Three old men, in local accent probably exaggerated so as to enable them to laugh at those French who don't understand it, asked if we were taking the *Chemin des Cathares*. Unfazed, we told them it was the GR 7 really. Just as, further west of here, all footpaths are *Route de Compostelle*, so here everything has to be *Cathare*: château, footpaths, camp sites, grottoes, furniture shops, even estate agents. Excellent walking in

Fourteenth century wooden arcades, *les couverts*, at Mirepoix

warm, even hot, sunshine. Black fig trees, where a shake of the stick caused dozens to fall, bursting with a fat splat as they hit the ground. Two praying mantises, partridges, butterflies. We picnicked peaceably in shade overlooking miles of rolling hills. But feeling at one with nature is a tricky concept. How can words express it, when – finite, classifying, rule-bound - they're what stands between us and it?

There was a long stony descent to the valley, and a dreary main road into Mirepoix. We trudged along in the heat as in a dream, our interest barely quickened even by Napoleonic milestones, and a live quail on the road. I moved it to the verge – it may just have been stunned by the draught of passing HGVs; birds that try for safety by flying low often get caught thus. Millennia of slow evolution are being subverted in a single generation. Into Mirepoix at last, a bastide, with fourteenth century wooden arcades – *les couverts* – round the main square. A young man passed, barefoot, a glittering bogey pinned to the side of his nose. Written in felt-tip on his sack was: '*Je vagabonde par un monde immonde*' (a wanderer in a dirty world). A comment to/on us? A reminder to him? A plea? No wonder people look oddly at walkers. A cat was stalking a dog in the town-centre. The dog walked with feigned unconcern, though turning sheepishly every now and then. About ten yards behind, the cat jumped from doorway to doorway, intent on its game. We dined in the hotel courtyard – still warm at 10pm. **24km**

Day 70: Difficulty finding letterbox and open bakery – Mirepoix was rather a surly place, we decided. GR 7 was along an old railway track. It was also a short-cut from the local college into town; we passed several groups of students, some sitting in the fields for a smoke, others in hazel coppices(!). The path then wound through some very pretty oak-woods, where Gaz de France has a pipeline – beautifully concealed, you'd never know it was there except for the notices. Then signs and map contradicted each other and we had to take a road for some kilometres into Lagarde. This was a village with an *Hôtel de Ville*, which is a step up from a *mairie*, but it had no shops at all. The church had an enthusiastic model-maker – there was a History of Christianity in models in every side-chapel, and more could be seen stored in the vestry. We picnicked in the square, then strolled down to the river, the Hers, a river which has a classic intermittent source, which sometimes interrupts its flow for two or three days. A plaque on the bridge recorded its opening in 1883 by the Senator for the Ariège and Mayor of Lagarde. His patronage must be the explanation of the *Hôtel de Ville*. House martins' phlegmy twittering as they gathered for migration. Then a station unmistakable even though abandoned, and more railway track. All rails and sleepers, signs and notices had been removed; all that remained was the bed, and the engineering – bridges, culverts etc. Without the sleepers it made for rather agreeable walking. Huguette winningly begged some water from two elderly men at a former crossing-keeper's cottage now a suburban villa. They were happy to talk about the railway, which ran from Bram to Lavelanet, and closed more than fifty years ago. We scrumped more figs along the track, before arriving in Camon on a quite spectacular viaduct above the river. Not very safe, after fifty years disuse, either.

Camon had one shop (with a very talkative owner), one tourist office (with a very laconic girl in charge), one café (closed, 'it's not the season'). But there was also an abbey-cum-château, fortified, with part of the village inside the precinct. This was one of the seven 'prettiest villages of France' that I went through, like St Céneri-le-Gérei on Day 25. The others were St Léon-sur-Vézère, Belvès, Monpazier, Bruniquel, Puycelci and Lautrec. The title is not awarded by a state body, but by the *collectivité* of prettiest villages – there are 140 at the time of writing. As well as being naturally pretty, they have to meet certain criteria about the maintenance of prettiness, financial commitment to being pretty, etc. Certainly those I saw were pretty by anyone's standards, though others (Fanjeaux, Montricoux, Villebois-Lavalette) were, I thought, their equal. But it's a good example of French society organising something without either help or interference from the central authority.

Short day, so we lounged on *café* benches, reading the paper in the shade, then left town past a machine for holding animals during shoeing. Straps under the belly and a hoist were used to suspend the animal, then its legs were tied to prevent kicking. Otherwise it took four or five strong men to hold it still. Up a one-in-four hill to the *chambre d'hôte*, which had a really fine view and offered every sort of accommodation – camp-site, caravans, chalets, as well as rooms. And it was a farm with animals, farm-shop etc. As we talked with M and Mme Dumons, their small grandson arrived to announce: 'The cow's dead.' 'OK, we'll call the knacker,' said M Dumons comfortably. Dinner outstanding: *charcuterie, civet de sanglier* (wild boar stew), cheese, dessert, any amount to drink. Another couple, from Marseille, about our age, who'd been staying for three or four days, helped keep the conversation rolling. It ranged over vegetables (quality, prices, idiosyncrasies of); mushrooms; beef (for thirty years French cows have had annual blood-tests and identity checks, though BSE has shown that cheating is possible); who should have called the electrician and didn't; hip replacements. Parsley, a notoriously capricious herb, should be planted by 'the one who wears the trousers'. So! **15km**

Day 71: Breakfast was as lively as supper. The Dumons' farm straddled two departments (and two regions indeed), so that calculating the taxes was a nightmare. Their solution to what seems to be a well-known

Beside the man-made lake at Montbel

problem was for the land in Aude (Languedoc-Roussillon) to be registered as hers, and that in Ariège (Midi-Pyrénées) to be his. They'd divided the inheritance among their three children so that the farm could be kept as a going concern by the eldest son (French law demands that children inherit equal shares). 'But the in-laws won't like it,' they muttered. *Oreillettes* – thin, crispy, sugary wafers, though here large and square, not ear-shaped – jam, croissants, lots of coffee.

We spotted the dead cow, legs up, behind a barn, waiting for the knacker and being inspected by a flock of anxious guinea-fowl. Walked back to Camon accompanied by the farm dog, which turned out to be on a visit to its friends in the village. Then the railway track again for a couple of miles, to a disused tunnel where, thankfully, the GR dodged to one side. Up through wood to farmland, here always on top. Suddenly there were chestnuts, woodlarks, sand underfoot. Down again to Montbel, and a man-made (1984) lake, which must be a beach, in season. Even now yachts could be seen on the far side, two people were swimming, other walkers were about. We crossed a dyke running between a constant level reservoir, and an ordinary one now rather low after the long dry spell. The pale grey sky, and the forests turning autumnal shades were reflected in the still water; we might have been in Finland or Canada, rather than southern France. A short cut took us through a shockingly sordid hamlet of three farms, several deserted houses and a church. There was manure everywhere, the main street was covered in slurry, old harrows, chickens, straw, baling-wire. In the surrounding fields were poultry, mud, rotting wood-piles, old cars. We picnicked an agreeable distance away. Across a ridge to the railway again, into Labastide, where our search for tonight's accommodation continued, helped by the grocer's wife and phone-book. We almost booked into a posh hotel which turned out to be more than ten miles from where we were aimed; but did book into a very ordinary hotel (with less ordinary prices). Lovely path in the afternoon through oaks on a ridge; woodmouse, red squirrel. We passed a sixteenth century chapel where, outside, a black woman was writing copious notes in the shade. The old part of Laroque d'Olmes is a hilltop fortified village; the main town has factories and houses sprawling along the main road – light industry especially textile-related, HGVs, a huge factory with a plume of blue smoke, our hotel. Huguette had an allergic reaction on her leg, above the sock, which was thought to be the cause. I suggested that putting the sock on her head would raise spots into a halo. Ouch! Noticed on writing up the day how the entries had tended to lengthen. Can this just be the practice? Is there in fact more to notice here than in Normandy? Or, more likely, is it that the perspectives and connections of a journey become easier to see as it progresses – one sees where one is going? **23km**

Day 72: A rather noisy night, what with a constant low drone from factory and early HGVs, but it was warm in the room; clean cold sunrise at 8 am. We arrived for breakfast spruce and neat. 'Haven't you got a car then?' said the manager, flabbergasted to learn we were walking. Over breakfast we were told that the factory makes fabric for car seats, exported all over Europe, and as far as the United States and Japan. Then a morning-dew start (it was September 28, after all), with the sun rising behind us, and easy waymarks. The first kilometres of the path had even been mown. After 5km or so a finger-post '*Sentier des Cathares*' (surprise, surprise), and almost immediately we were lost. The waymarks were old and overgrown, new tracks seemed to have been made everywhere. We developed a system – leave the sacks at the last certain waymark, each take one branch, call when we pick up the track, go back for the sacks. Very slow progress, obviously. After several of these, we found we were following yellow-and-white flashes, or even yellow alone, instead of the red-and-yellow we had started with. Made wrong choices, blundered about in long grass, brambles, and frustration. Followed horse-track in the wrong direction (I knew we should be going west), and found a tremendous view northwards from top of cliffs. The path bent inexorably east. Should we try a cross-country route? Cliffs put us off. So we re-traced steps. We had two maps and a guide, which gave three different routes. Decided on lunch to clear our minds. As we sat down there was a huge soft whoomp just behind us. I jumped up to see something drop to the ground in trees twenty yards away. Alarmed inspection showed a Goshawk flying off, and a Rock Dove minus lots of feathers twitching direly on the ground. The further shock of me examining its legs to see if it was ringed made it struggle to its wings and flop into a nearby bush.

Consulting good clear signs

Further retracing of steps brought us back to the path after three wasted hours. Even armed with this experience we lost the almost invisible waymarks twice more, before suddenly finding we were through the gap in the cliffs and descending towards a village. Huguette took on water at a feeding-trough containing two goldfish. One house in the village, painted a pale yellow, was covered with a soggy mass of slow-droning big flies. This didn't mean it contained a corpse – I know of other houses that produce flies. It may be the colour that attracts them, but what do they eat and breed on? Then more descent, far too much indeed, as the next climb was shattering. In all this region, the foothills of the Pyrenees run in parallel east-west ridges, each a little higher than the last. On the south-facing slope, the *soulane* or *adret*, there are fields, villages, crops, gardens; the north-facing slope, the *bac*, or *ubac*, is colder, wetter, more forested, less cultivated, less inhabited; the vegetation is different; even the birds aren't the same. So we struggled up a one-in-six slope, over 3km of it, in dense dripping sunless forest. Panting and exhausted, we reached the grassland at the top, then suddenly, within five yards, we were on the ridge, 300m above the next valley, with views for 50km and a castle, *'precipice-encurled'*, on our left. Further towards the east could be seen a rocky pinnacle, the *pog* of Montségur crowned by another ruined castle. This really is a *château cathare.* In 1243 a group of Cathars under Pierre-Roger of Mirepoix, including their last French bishop and many of their élite, the *perfecti* or *parfaits*, was besieged here by the Catholic Crusaders. After a siege of nine months they surrendered. More than 200 men and women were burnt on a bonfire at the foot of the rock. The site of the bonfire can still be seen. Although individuals, groups, and even one or two strongholds, still resisted, this marked the end of Catharism as a religion with a coherent doctrine and a directing hierarchy.

Now, of course, the path went just as steeply down as it had up. We stumbled through the village of Roquefixade, and down the road to our *gîte*, by now completely shattered walkers with twitching knees. Another party in the *gîte,* a group of eight, old acquaintances, aged from thirty to seventy. They were here with an organisation which specializes in walking holidays where your baggage is bussed from one halt to the next, while you can walk or not. They advertise holidays 'organised, guided, or on your own'. Eh? The group was paying more than we were, I'm glad to say. At dinner they talked with volcanic enthusiasm, three or four at once, some keen to ask about UK attitudes (to the euro, for example) or us personally. One, and there always is one, made the traditional jokes – Brits trying to book rooms in the *Hôtel de Ville* (have you heard the one about French tourists trying to buy slippers in Boots?), how a pretty English teacher threw him out of class for confusing 'beach' and 'bitch'. Oh sure. Convivial meal, mainly the home-grown produce of the couple in charge – tomato salad, rabbit stew, potatoes and beans. Madame regaled the horrified group with tales of her delinquent daughter-in-law, and her delinquent and appalling grand-daughter. The family honour was safe in other hands: a ten-year-old grandson had filled the mantelpiece with VTT (cross-country cycling) trophies. **21km** – is that all?

Day 73: We set off with everyone's good wishes into a low mist. Madame showed us a short cut and took the opportunity to scathe the other group: 'Not real walkers – did you see how many bags they've got? At least three each.' Road, then a clearly marked track, past a farm about as isolated as it's possible to be without falling right off the edge, then a well-marked path along the top of the ridge, the Plantaurel, cloud down and visibility nil. Heavy, dripping forest; under beech and box it was still night. The rain thickened to a steady downpour. We were soaked, despite waterproofs, and frozen too. Along forest track for hours thinking we'd missed the path, then met two other walkers looking for somewhere we'd never heard of (later we realised they'd misunderstood the signs and had overshot by kilometres). Out of the trees on to a grassy plateau. Down below, places we know were in sight – Montgailhard, supermarkets, the dam at Mercus. To the north, we could see the next (lower) ridge, with the reservoir of La Barre between.

Many French towns have a place-name La Barre or La Barrière. Dieppe had one, I noticed. They mark the sites of the *octroi*, local customs offices that collected taxes from incoming goods. Mediæval London had similar sites, eg Temple Bar. The *octroi* was introduced in France in the thirteenth century; some offices survived, amazingly, until 1948, despite the system's clumsiness, cost (up to fifty per cent of the receipts) and unpopularity. The '*taxes locales*' of some towns, still levied on certain goods and services, like tourism, are what replaced the *octroi* when it was finally abolished.

Rain was replaced by freezing wind. We missed the path again. Wasted less than an hour today getting it right, by finding a farm, though threatened by dogs, and asking. Two gnarled and unshaven farmers showed us the track, and advised us: 'These two dogs are no trouble, but if the brown one gets behind you, it'll bite. Just give it a thump with your stick.' They were in much more serious trouble than

Mountain stream in the Ariège

we were: the next day was *la Saint-Michel*, the big sheep-market in Tarascon, and the rain, wet clay and a bogged-down tractor had immobilised their transport and their sheep. The serious buying and selling takes place well before dawn on these occasions, so they had to get their flock off the mountain before dark.

On the path down we met two more walkers, with umbrellas – was this intelligent rambling or plain amateur? After seven hours' walking with virtually no stop because of the rain, Huguette had a serious muscle strain in her thigh, and we descended slowly. A shelter under an overhanging rock, which some optimist had provided with walls, offered just enough room for the two of us to eat a sandwich in the dry. Finally arrived in Foix, physically and emotionally exhausted, and needing hot chocolate and shandy chasers to revive. Foix was a mediæval County; circumstances and remoteness kept it independent until 1607, one of the last regions to be acquired by the French Crown. The best-known of the Counts was Gaston III (1331-1391). He was quite untypical of the Middle Ages, more of a Renaissance prince. He adopted the name of Fébus (Phoebus, Greek god of the sun and hunting). A brilliant ruler, author of a treatise on hunting (one of his hunting lodges can still be seen at Siguer), it is he who is supposed to have written the Pyrenean love-song I sang on Day 65. But, passionate, turbulent, authoritarian, he had his brother assassinated and, like Ivan the Terrible, killed his only son. It's via the County of Foix that the French President is one of the two co-princes of Andorra (the other is the Bishop of La Seu d'Urgell, in Spain). The castle of the Counts, plain but functional, still dominates the town. I came through here in 1956, why didn't I know all this then? Something to do with being eighteen, perhaps. Then, the town was dozing in the heat of early August as we visited the castle. Afterwards, we hitched a lift southwards in a 2CV. The fabric roof was rolled back to let the driver stand up at frequent intervals to whistle at pretty girls. His companion, who was a friar, or at least dressed in a habit, smiled indulgently. There was much more traffic in the town than then, but the opening of a tunnel in 2001 was to take much of it away and allow the town (with 10,000 inhabitants, the smallest county-town in France) to revert to its provincial sleepiness.

We separated at the station – Huguette to spend the weekend with her sister in Toulouse, I to cover the rougher terrain of the remaining three days. As I pursued the road towards *my chambre d'hôte*, I met three old friends on the way – it turned out they live here. They didn't recognise me at first in hat, cape and sack. When I finally reached it, the *chambre d'hôte* in Ganac was welcoming and warm. I spread wet gear on every hot-water pipe, and dried out. Dinner was a tin of mackerel, bread-and-cheese, chocolate - very healthy, I'm sure. At night, I kept thinking it was raining, but it was the noise of the little stream a few feet away. This room used to be a forge; Ganac had a series of little water-driven forges, all specializing in making nails. **21km**

Day 74: Breakfast with Monsieur, who was very keen on driving – that is with carriage and horses, Duke of Edinburgh style – not the local breed of horse, the *Mérens*, but the *Comté*, from Franche-Comté in eastern France, like the cheese. Off-road when tracks were suitable; some time he'd like to go to Compostella in this way. Hard start to the 900m (3,000ft) climb was made easier by a made road to a hamlet. After thirty minutes I completed 1,000 miles! That made it easier too. The first farm had no fewer than sixty-eight plaques for national cattle-show participation, late '70s and early '80s. The hamlet was more of a village really; two inhabitants apologised for their aggressive dog, showed me the track. It was very steep and every time I stopped to blow, which was often, the view took away what breath I had. Toulouse, more than 80km away; the Montagne Noire, where I had finished in June; all the last seven days' walk; Montségur standing up dark and uncompromising. I paused at a forest track. As it was Saturday, everyone was out – shots, shouts, barks. Along the track came three four-wheel drives in convoy. What adventure could they think they were having? Two cyclists came down the path as I tackled the forest with an eye out for mushrooms. Leaning my chin on the stick for breath, I saw a *cèpe* (penny bun) within a foot of mine. And on the grassy summit were parasol mushrooms ignored by the groups of motorists who were looking for crystals by the roadside. So I took my legal maximum of three kilos. That evening I gave them to Mme Robert

Pyrenees, above *la mer des nuages*

at the *chambre d'hôte*. Passed other men looking for *cèpes*, and a party of ten men having a picnic – fire, grill, *apéritif*, tables, chairs. What did they tell their wives? From the top, the main chain of the Pyrenees had become visible; much in cloud, though, and an alarming quantity of fresh snow. After the vision on Day 65 I was fated not to see my favourite summits again. Hot sun, cold wind, occasional clouds – I spent much time changing clothes. Down to Saurat in the valley to phone. Tomorrow's *gîte*, the last overnight stop of the whole trek, had just been sold, and was closed. So I'd anti-climax down in the main valley, and re-jig the route. Saurat, with 600 inhabitants, had two groceries, a café, a tobacconist, a priest, two telephone boxes, a chemist, a school, an industry (well, one man making sharpening-stones), two shepherds; it was still (just) a viable village. In the shop where I bought a drink, I was regarded with overt suspicion – would I leave my sack by the cash-desk and not take it behind the shelves. Please. I found later that there was a growing community of drop-outs, not well-considered by the locals. Two passed as I sat on the square quenching my thirst. But hey! Where were my dreadlocks, my nose-ring, my army-surplus gear, my bedraggled moll? No, stick, boots and unfamiliarity were enough.

Over dinner with M and Mme Robert, talk touched intelligently on French administration, pensions, teachers' conditions of work (they're civil servants in France, with the special status – unsackability etc – that goes with that). M Robert was a big wheel in the rambling world, chairing committees to set up footpaths etc, and brought a usefully outside view. He had worked in Morocco for more than twenty years. The Roberts used to run the nearby *gîte d'étape*, since closed. He despaired at the French inability to change. Tradition is a term of unqualified approval. We swapped 'habit' stories – holidays in August for the gregarious French; midday meal at 12.00 for the convivial French, especially on Sundays; drive where you're going on Sunday because that's what you've always done, even when retirement allows you to avoid the jams; schools closing for a day in mid-week despite child-minding problems for working mothers. Forty-eight per cent of the French are against the clock-changes in spring and autumn, with regular claims that it takes two to three weeks to get accustomed,

Field of autumn crocus

and rumours that it is due to be abandoned 'next year' (though jet-lag causes no more problems than to Brits). Claret is still graded on the 1855 classification. And what about the euro? People even of my age still talk in 'old' francs, ie those of before the currency changes of 1959 (1000 old ones = 10 new ones). However will they manage when 10 francs (1000 old francs) = 7.63 euros? It was scheduled to happen in January 2002, but despite huge publicity, and everything being labelled in both currencies, there were increasing wishful rumours that the change would not take place at all. An interesting and convivial evening.

There were three squashed salamanders on today's almost deserted roads, and yet another dead shrew on the path – do they seek out the GR to die? Do so many die that these are a genuine statistical sample? Do they lie around because no scavenger likes the taste? Whole fields of autumn crocus – in one place a small copse was so thickly carpeted they might have been bluebells. Autumn colours were coming on beech and bracken; in two weeks or less they'd be a rich golden-brown brocade on the hillsides. **20km**

Day 75: Short and anti-climactic day. Disagreeable drizzle and surprisingly steep climb up valley side to Cabus. There used to be a school here, and the solidly-built buildings are still in good nick. But there is only one permanently inhabited house now; all the others are holiday homes. The weather improved and the track was well-marked and soft underfoot. I decided to visit Bédeilhac, where there was a *café* and a cave. Anything was better than spending six hours on a sad Sunday in Tarascon. Though it was not very exciting here either, I must say. Another lot of hounds in a cage outside farm were barking piteously for passers-by to take them for a walk. The *café* turned out to be restaurant, so I stayed for meal, but hopes of conviviality were dashed – the only other guests were a girl and her granny. The grandmother kept asking the girl (about ten or twelve) if she needed help cutting her meat; the girl behaved impeccably in not screaming. Why can't the French let their children grow up? They do their homework for them, choose their courses and careers for them, buy their cars and their flats for them. At no age are the children guaranteed freedom and responsibility. A twenty-five-year-old civil servant with a good job in the Ministry of Defence may be asked by a landlord to have his rent guaranteed by his parents. My personal impression is that this dead hand of control is gaining ground, too. And as parents to children, so state to citizens, some might say.

After a good but silent lunch, to Grotte de Bédeilhac, the biggest in this part of the world (though Niaux has far finer relics). The cave is big enough to have been used for aircraft repair and storage before and during World War II. Photos of a plane taking off and landing inside the cave mouth are a post-war stunt, though. But mightily impressive. There is a walk of a kilometre into a chamber of stalactites and stalagmites left from heaven knows when – the cave was made by rushing underground water. Then there's evidence of earthquakes, an uncomfortable thought so far from the entrance. The prehistory traces are less impressive, having been pillaged long ago by local souvenir hunters. But they were made the most of by our informed and informative guide. The cave was the scene of an artistic administrative farce a few years ago. The Minister of Culture had a bed set up in the cave, in which artists spent the night with a view to being inspired; with quite other views in some cases, say the locals. No artistic works inspired by this are known, although £2,500 was spent in subsidies. The others in the group were a family of four Americans from Toulouse, where he was working in space research. All four spoke good French. They reckoned they could spend forever just visiting the interesting places within reach of Toulouse.

Outside again, the path had two notices. One said: 'Danger. No Entry'; the other: 'Follow yellow waymarks'. My law-abiding soul brought me to a halt, torn. In the end I decided that this was typically French in its insistence on regulation, but that the loophole for individual initiative should be encouraged. There is no French word for 'law-abiding'. This is not to say that the idea cannot be expressed in

French – simply that it's not a concept basic enough to be conveyed in a single word. And '*respectueux des lois*' doesn't carry any connotation of approval, as ' a law-abiding citizen' does in English. The French concept of law is of something imposed, rather than of something consented to. There's a constant struggle between the State, which tries to control, and the citizens, who try to do what they like. To an English eye, the proliferation of laws and regulations is astonishing: legislation decrees which drinks can be sold on credit, the number of chemists' shops and taxis in each town, how much time must elapse before a widow may remarry (300 days), what menus a restaurant must post outside (and for how long), who inherits how much (no leaving your all to a cattery, or your best mate, or one child of your seven), the 152 – is it? – chemicals that may be added to wine. You may not pick mushrooms at night, or address your pig as Napoleon. All couples must have a medical before marrying (though the results can't stop them). And this is a relaxation. Twenty years ago the price of a baguette was fixed, funerals were a state monopoly, all foreigners had to register for overnight stays. Nor are these laws merely dead-letters, like Brits having to practise archery on Sunday, etc.

But as individuals, the French deeply distrust all organs of the State. State monopolies and politicians may be, and are, prosecuted for corruption, but nobody is shocked. 'We've put you there to provide, promote, protect, not to tell us what to do,' is the attitude, and getting round, or simply ignoring unpopular laws is a national pastime.

This combination of public *dirigisme* and private anarchy can be a successful recipe; relations with the outside world always have this double perspective, and politicians cleverly shift focus from one to the other. This often looks to more straightforward Brits as if the French were having their cake and eating it – 'French *gâteau* is the best in the world: the more you eat, the more there is left'.

The current campaign against junk food – *la malbouffe* – has national approval. Ministers refer respectfully to the campaign leader, José Bové; thousands turn out to hear him speak. Yet millions of the French eat at McDonald's, pizzas are as popular as in the UK, the summer roads are lined with chippies. All the customers believe, and will say, that French cooking is the best in the world even while they're ingesting this stuff.

They don't even visit their best restaurants that much. Forty-five per cent of visitors to Michelin-starred restaurants are foreigners. Their ideal would be to have stringent laws against junk food, but to carry on as now.

They can even be heard boasting that the unique strength of French society lies in this ability to make laws and not observe them. 'Speed limit? What speed limit?' 'Seat-belts? What seat-belts?' More than thirty per cent of French traffic offences never get to court because of pressures exerted, favours called in, strings pulled. No wonder the police find foreign drivers a softer touch – no friends in the Town Hall means a quick, straightforward case.

Another result is on relationships between individuals. In any difference – land boundaries, inheritances, noisy neighbours etc – the law/police are constantly solicited, and as constantly abused (in both senses). Of course, once you have a society in which any discord means recourse to the law, negotiating skills have little value. Express your individuality and let the chips fall where they may.

Where was I, now? Oh yes, criticising French officialdom for stifling individual initiative? French individualism for not recognising its limits? Or encouraging French individualism by choosing which official notice I preferred to obey? Hm. Yes. Well. Er. I slipped and fell on the 'dangerous' path while thus reflecting, and it was far longer than the map showed. Two further reasons for the nasty attack of tetchiness that set in for the remaining miles.

The hotel in Tarascon had an amazingly animated life for a Sunday evening, usually as dead a time as you can get. The bar was full of youngish men watching football – a league match. The restaurant was full too – several middle-aged couples and a larger group of young people, including a baby; all looked about fourteen, except for one balding loud-mouth, who behaved as if he were fourteen. The baby didn't look fourteen either, but was a decidedly social creature. It did all the right things – leering uncontrollably at the waitress, letting itself be chucked under the chin, spasmodically banging the flat of its fat hands on the table, seizing the cloth in a relentless fist. **17km**

Day 76: Rain, rain, low cloud, cold, rain. Had made the best of the change of plan compelled by the closure of the final *gîte d'étape*, but it would mean a good deal of road-walking on this final day. This passed uneventfully. I climbed 300m to the village of Lapège to rejoin the planned route. Lapège is a living museum; until recently – the 1950s – they were still using the swing-plough, an implement that simply scratches the soil without turning it over as the plough-share does. Romans would have recognised it straightaway. The path runs along the *soulane* on a gallery joining the high-level villages of this side. It's called the *camin de nobios* (lovers'walk), I believe because, in summer at least, the rocks give out the sun's stored heat until well into the night. No chance of that today, though. Occasional paroxysms of drizzle, oddly enough when I'd just removed my waterproof. A cold wind flexed its muscles too. I passed a number of barns, used for storing hay and for livestock over winter. One was open and still had a sprig of box nailed to a beam. This is the plant blessed in church on Palm Sunday (as pussy willow in parts of the UK, there being no palms there either); it is then hung in the barns to protect the animals, or tucked into the collars of the bell-wethers when the flocks set out on the spring *transhumance* to the mountain pastures.

Down in the valley at the crossroads but clearly visible from here, 300m above, is a monument to Theophile Delcassé – *'ce grand Français'* – MP for the Ariège, and Foreign Minister. Within weeks of being appointed he had to give way to the British over Fashoda, still resented by some French as a climb-down, as I had found on Day 10. But, clear-sighted and resolute, tenacious and energetic, and a determined opponent of any fundamental agreement with Germany, he was the French mover of the *Entente Cordiale* of 1904. After much behind-the-scenes diplomacy, the visit of Edward VII to Paris at the beginning of May 1903 was the perfect setting for this agreement ending the enmities, rivalries, and some of the misunderstandings, of centuries. But it was 'a damned near-run thing'. Britain and France had almost fought on two or three occasions in the 1890s, and despite the personal popularity of the king, the cheers from the crowds lining the streets were matched and even drowned by the whistles and boos. But a lavish programme of entertainment and spectacle, and the limitless and evident good humour of the francophile king won the Parisians round. By the third day they were cheering him to the echo, while the few protesters found themselves disclaimed, shouted at, and hustled away. A visit to London by the French President Emile Loubet and Delcassé was greeted with an equal English enthusiasm. The *Entente* which followed the new cordiality, finally ratified on April 8, 1904, allowed solutions to a number of long-standing disagreements, especially in the two colonial empires. It also ended the isolation of both countries within Europe. Because of this *Entente*, we fought on the same side in two world wars. Because of this, Churchill, in June 1940, could offer political union of the two countries. Because of this, two temperamentally opposed countries have been on speaking terms and better for the whole of the twentieth century. We're each other's mirrors, mirrors in which we both see our secret fears and phobias have been turned into a functioning social structure by people who see no reason to be afraid. There *is* no reason to be afraid. Despite the differences in our societies, laws, public life, outlook, attitudes, expectations, and despite occasional tantrums as at French lorry-drivers or BSE, it's now possible for us to respect each other as equals. A great Frenchman indeed. However, Delcassé's name now is a dead-letter in France, barely making it into the footnotes of history books. In nearby Pamiers, his birthplace, the new lycée was recently refused permission to adopt his name (cp Day 20). I hope the centenary will receive proper acknowledgement on both sides of the Channel.

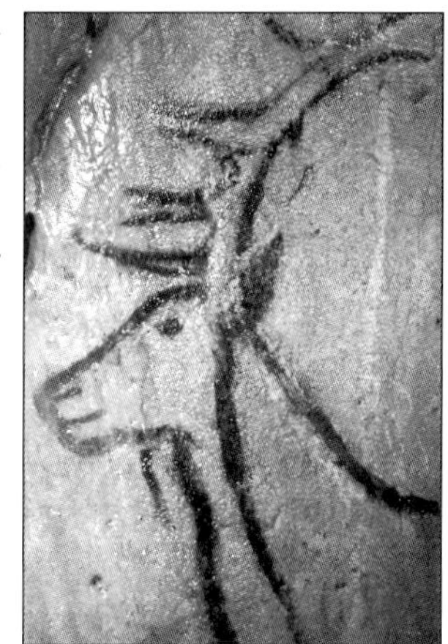

Cave painting at the Grotte de Niaux

Also visible, just beyond the same crossroads indeed, was the village of Siguer where one of the hunting lodges of Gaston Fébus can still be seen. It is also the village of the French sprint champion, Claude Piquemal, gold medallist at the European games of 1962. The whole village went wild when he won, and no doubt you can be shown his house too. On the other side of the valley too, is the Grotte de Niaux, one of the few sites still open for seeing original cave-paintings. And there are the iron-mines of the Rancié that were the main wealth of the valley from 'time

Goulier: the church in cloud

immemorial' until 1930. Mining was the monopoly of three villages; so jealously did the miners guard their right to mine the ore where and how they wished, that it was impossible to take the necessary safety precautions. Finally the roof of the last gallery fell in, killing three men and putting the whole enterprise out of business.

I spent ten minutes trying to squeeze into the shelter of an overhanging rock, but the rain stopped first. Across the valley, the Pique d'Endron (2473m) towered into the cloud above Goulier. Nearly there! I ate a last sandwich, jettisoned my remaining rations then descended through acacia woods. In May they would be frosty with the bunches of white flowers; in June the falling petals would make creamy drifts along roads and paths. Now they were shedding translucent lemon and pure hair-brown leaves; this is the *soulane*. On the north-facing slope opposite, the trees were still a dull green, except for the yellowing birches. Hot chocolate and twenty minutes rest in Vicdessos café, where I mulled over the whole enterprise, remembering the people I'd met, the conversations, the army of ghosts – prehistoric, Roman, mediæval, modern – who had accompanied my steps, the landscapes. Then the historical figures who'd come alive: Mersenne, Chanzy, the Saumur cadets, Mistral, Rousseau, Riquet, the Cathars and St Dominic, Delcassé. And what about all the things I'd missed? I was visited by the gloomy thought that the last step of a journey may be even harder than the first. Then up the final climb, another 300m, by the old track where possible.

Does the road wind up-hill all the way?
Yes, to the very end.

At five past four I marched, grinning triumphantly in the rain, up by the side of the church, up the deserted village street, and home, not just to Christina Rossetti's roof and bed, but to champagne and Huguette. **24km**

The end of the journey – celebrating with the support teams, Chris and George Hart on the left, Huguette on the right

ENDRON

It was already late when I set out
(Anorak, hat, suncream glucose),
I strode up with a rush through the gardens
Where bees ere bouncing a night-numbed rose
And frumping the dahlias about;
The tiny uproar of insects and martins
Petering out

As I stepped on up towards where the hills
Shrug off their clinging shawl of pines
Lushness and soil. Upwards there's no end
To the rise and rise of rockier skylines,
But the steady-falling beck reveals
The constant even pressure to descend
That hugs my heels,

Ever more clearly, in the dull trudge
Zig zag zig zag across the slopes.
The mountain's shrinking to disappearance,
Scarcity is its new emblem, my hopes,
The sign of progress. At last the ridge:
(A fly whines into the sudden distance)
But still the peaks judge

Unfavourably! I plod above those
Blue, already sun-abandoned, combes,
Tackle the long slow slog to the height
Where up finishes for ever, and becomes
Past! Then I've made it! Looking shows
A consummation of unhindered light,
Mountains in rows,

Prim, unsuspected tarns; the muscular shot
Of achievement re-orders the whole world;

I sign the Livre d'Or, sprawl on the summit
Laughing, gulping my breath back, getting cold,
Wondering whether to stay or not;
Patient rocks in the last sunshine plummet,
Distant doors shut

As that pure elated stab refuses
To be caught again. Now everywhere is down.
Will that be all then? Will I sink
To nothing? To potter in my dressing-gown,
To suck my teeth and peer through glasses,
To think whatever old men think
When a girl passes.

USES FOR A STICK

Walking (especially up steep slopes)

Keeping dogs off

Breaking cobwebs

Bashing nettles, brambles etc

Drying clothes on

Measuring snakes

Sounding mud/water

As a balancing pole

Security (wedged against suspect hotel door; burglar alarm)

Impersonating a pilgrim or scout master

Alerting on-coming drivers (especially round blind bends)

Prop for standing still while getting stones out of shoe etc

Newt-tickling

'Crucifixion'-walking, to relieve swollen hands and air armpits

Wedging windows open to ensure cool breeze

Recreational, eg baton-twirling, balancing, flipping fallen branches out of the way

Squailing (knocking fruit, nuts etc off trees)

Talking to (though I never had to try this)

USEFUL INFORMATION

Where to stay – You may be ambitious, tough and young enough to carry a tent, and keep strictly to the GR, but there are sections of over 40km with no accommodation available, and short-cuts, detours etc may be preferable.
Hotels – The red *Guide Michelin* gives good information, but omits many hotels, especially the simpler, cheaper ones. Departmental Tourist Boards may provide complete lists, but often seem to assume that all British tourists are wealthy, or they provide information only on hotels that have sponsored them. Try:

www.tourisme.fr
www.france-bonjour.fr

Chambres d'hôte – Bed-and-Breakfast *à la française*. The organisation Gîtes de France publishes an annual list (don't confuse the *chambres d'hôte* with the *Gîtes Ruraux*, which are for renting, not overnight stays). I found the guide helpful and accurate. There are other organisations with similar lists. Some, though not all, serve evening meals.

www. gites-de-france.fr
www. likhom. com
www.hotes-en-france.com

Walkers' hostels – There's no umbrella organisation, but Annick and Serge Mouraret publish a guide *Gîtes d'étape. Refuges*, which gives all hostels known to the authors. I found it rather inaccurate (two listed had been closed for two years, and a third was unwilling to open for one walker). But other information was correct, and sensible walkers, who will anyway be telephoning in advance, will be adequately served.

www.gites-refuges.com

Guides – The Fédération Française de Randonnées Pédestres (FFRP)

www.ffrp.asso.fr

which is responsible for designating, maintaining, and waymarking the French footpaths, publishes *topoguides* to many paths. These contain large-scale maps, directions, descriptions of things of interest, details of accommodation, buses, trains, where to buy provisions, etc. They're obtainable in big French bookshops, and from Stanfords, Longacre, London.

I used 202 Pays de Caux, 312 Caen to Alençon, 321 Angoulême to Cahors, 323 Cahors to Albi. This left several gaps – from Le Havre to Ouistreham, P142 may help, if it's out yet. D203 covers the GR2 along the Seine. Alençon to Le Mans was out of print at the time of writing. Between Le Mans and Angoulême an enormous gap has no *topoguide* at all, but is well signposted and way-marked north of the Pyrenees, the Chemins de St Jacques de Compostelle, and the GR 10 are so popular that paths and guides are almost all east-west, and very few north-south. Depending on exactly where you wish to cross the Pyrenees, you may find *topoguides* 1097, 1090, 1092, and P651 useful. As well as their weight, *topoguides* have a few other drawbacks: they're directional - it's not always easy to find the way reading in reverse; one or two sections seemed to me to have been based on the map, rather than on the ground. But it's certainly worth reading them before you start.

Maps – You'll have to rely on these in many places, such as the gaps mentioned above. The green IGN Serie Verte (1: 100 000) is the best. Those I used were: 7 Dieppe-Caen, 18 Caen-Alençon, 19 Alençon-Le Mans, 25 Le Mans-Saumur, 33 Saumur-Niort, 39 Niort-Angoulême, 47 Angoulême-Périgueux, 48 Périgueux-Belvès, 57 Belvès-Caussade, 64 Puycelci-Castelnaudary, 71 Castelnaudary-end.
French footpaths are well waymarked on the whole (by volunteers) though it's still possible to get lost.

Minitel – One reason that the French have fewer publicly accessible internet facilities, than, say, Mexico, has been the huge success of Minitel, a database accessible by telephone. You can use it free at post offices, and may find these addresses useful;

3615 Cadolc (for *gîtes d'étape*)
3615 Itirando (information and suggestions)
3617 Météo (weather forecasts)

Mobiles – Check that yours will operate in France, before you go. On the whole, there are bigger areas of France – that wide, empty, countryside is one reason for such good walking - without mobile coverage. But this is constantly improving.

Money – Many of the *chambres d'hôte* and smaller hotels will not accept credit cards.

Acknowledgements

In addition to those thanked in the main text, I would like to thank the following: Al and Dorothy Shtasel, for recommending the GR 36, and giving me the *topoguides*; O'Byrne and Co for photographs and publicity; Jeremy Malies for constant critical encouragement; Christine and George Hart for putting me up as I shuttled through Paris, for their back-up and company and photographs; Marion and Thierry Maurel for their study floor; the FFRP representatives for Charente Maritime, Charente and Sarthe; Chris Baxter for advice and reassurance.

Also, all those who stood me a drink: M Brou, the van-driver in Gonneville, Mme Hamandjian-Blanchard, M Gaborit, M and Mme Holstein, M and Mme Thil-Toussaint, M and Mme Bouchard, M Salle, Mme Gaignard, M and Mme Dumons, M and Mme Robert as well as hoteliers in Montreuil-Bellay, Aulnay and Tournon d'Agenais whose names I did not learn; everyone who enjoyed a conversation, and the innumerable people who helped me find the way.

I've acknowledged most quotations in the text, but some not:

p106 G M Hopkins from *Duns Scotus Oxford*

p109 R Frost from *Stopping by Woods on a Sunny Evening*

p122 T S Eliot from *East Coker*

Oliver Andrew read Modern Languages (French and Russian) at Oxford, then taught in Welwyn Garden City, The Gambia and Brighton for thirty-five years. He is married, with two children, and he and his wife Huguette are now grandparents. His interests include reading, walking, poetry, bird-watching, philately, chess, history, vegetable-growing and genealogy. More than one hundred of his poems have been published in a variety of British journals.